Francis Peter de Labillière

Federal Britain

Unity and Federation of the Empire

Francis Peter de Labillière

Federal Britain
Unity and Federation of the Empire

ISBN/EAN: 9783337320843

Printed in Europe, USA, Canada, Australia, Japan

Cover: Foto ©Suzi / pixelio.de

More available books at **www.hansebooks.com**

FEDERAL BRITAIN;

OR,

UNITY AND FEDERATION OF THE EMPIRE.

BY

F. P. de LABILLIERE,

BARRISTER-AT-LAW OF THE MIDDLE TEMPLE, FELLOW OF THE
ROYAL COLONIAL INSTITUTE,
AND AUTHOR OF
"EARLY HISTORY OF THE COLONY OF VICTORIA."

WITH CHAPTER ON IMPERIAL DEFENCE

BY

MAJOR SIR GEORGE S. CLARKE, R.E., K.C.M.G.

" Incomparably the greatest question which we can discuss."
PROFESSOR SIR J. R. SEELEY.

LONDON:
SAMPSON LOW, MARSTON & COMPANY,
LIMITED,
St. Dunstan's House,
FETTER LANE, FLEET STREET, E.C.
1894.

INTRODUCTION.

For about a quarter of a century the all-important question, how the British Empire is to stand in the future—for none but degenerate Britons could be content to think of its fall—has been more and more engaging the interest and consideration of our people in all our great countries, both old and new. During this period I have followed the discussion of the subject, with the keen interest of one born and brought up in the Colonies, but resident for years in England. Thus, having been able to view the situation from both standpoints, I am convinced that the noblest form of patriotism is that which, whilst ever keeping a man's affections constant to his native land, is wide-minded and large-hearted enough to make him also deeply love all the old and new British lands beyond it—in a word, the Empire.

Such a blending of Provincial and Imperial sympathies is in perfect harmony, both with particular and general interests, which are common in so many great questions ; whilst those concerns, of minor importance, which are at all divergent, would be far from improved by a policy of separation.

Strongly influenced by such considerations, I have during the course of the discussion, from time to time, done my little best to advocate the cause nearest my heart, contributing—principally for discussion at the Royal Colonial Institute—papers on the subject of Imperial Unity and Federation; and, now, I venture to bring these together, believing that—as each deals with different parts of the question, so as to be really one of a series—they may usefully be combined as chapters in one volume. Among them I have introduced others required for the fuller treatment of the subject. I believe that the reproduction of these isolated efforts may also be of some benefit, in indicating the sequence of ideas by which thoughtful men—starting with a firm belief, that the permanent unity of the Empire is most desirable—cannot but inevitably arrive at the conclusion that the ultimate political bond of that union must be Federation.

Empire, Dominions and Provinces going hand in hand, will ever feel that they have the surest support from each other. Imperialism will never lessen a man's interest in Provincial concerns. I may be allowed to mention that, during all the long time I have been devoted to the former, I have never been unmindful of the latter—spending some years in searching out and writing the early history of my native Colony, and being at one time a member of a London vestry, and at another of a rural Local Board. Provincialism of the true kind will always be most effectively safeguarded—in pursuing its own best interests, in conducting its own self-government, without fear of external attack or interference—by the strength of Imperialism. There is, however, Provincialism and Provincialism. That of the "Little England" type cannot be too strongly condemned. Wherever it is to be found, all the Empire over, it means narrowness, pettiness, ignorance, prejudice. Its adherents in the great lands of Canada, Australia, and British Africa would even belittle them—making them comparatively small—by detaching and isolating them from the greatness of the Empire. Happily, however, smallness in numbers as well as in everything else, is everywhere the mark of the " Little Britain " school of thought or thoughtlessness.

Those who believe in British Federalism are, by some, regarded as enthusiastic optimists. For my part, I can only discover in the direction of that policy a view of the future of our Empire free from any shade of pessimism.

Though speeches, pamphlets, articles in magazines and newspapers, have appeared in abundance in all parts of the Empire, and have done a vast amount of good in promoting the great cause, it is remarkable that scarcely a book has been published on the Unity and Federation of the Empire. Professor Seeley's great work, the "Expansion of England," has rendered invaluable service, in drawing powerful historical conclusions in favour of the maintenance of unity; but no book has recently appeared, at all comprehensively, treating of that question in conjunction with Federation, except Mr. George R. Parkin's, published in 1892. Another valuable work, the first with the same name, Sir Frederick Young's " Imperial Federation," appeared in 1876. Mr. Jehu Mathew's, " A Colonist on the Colonial Question," also ably dealt with Federation, in 1872.

All possible arrangements and understandings for carrying out joint objects and for promoting the greatest harmony in the relations of the Empire, especially as to trade and tariffs, must command the sympathy of all true Federalists; but if Federation can bestow nothing else, it—and it alone—can confer on commerce the greatest of advantages—perfect security and freedom from interference, especially safe transit across the seas. Every Federalist, however much further he may wish to go, can heartily endorse the following declaration of principles, in regard to the commerce and unity of the Empire, drawn up by Sir Charles Tupper, whom I have to thank for kindly giving me leave to insert it in these pages—

1. "That the best interests of Great Britain and of the outlying portions of the Empire alike, demand the permanent maintenance of the connection between them.

2. "That the promotion of the closest intercourse by trade arrangements, steamships, postal and cable communications between the different Colonies, and between them and the Mother Country, will increase the development of the Colonies, expand the trade, and promote the permanent unity of the Empire.

3. "That the duty incumbent upon every portion of the Empire to contribute to the defence of the Empire, will be promoted by bringing the Imperial Government into the most intimate possible relation with those of Canada, Australasia and South Africa."

British commerce must stand or fall with Imperialism, which, if it cannot arrange fiscal affairs as traders wish, can carry the flag before, and hold it over, them on land and sea, and that is doing very much. That "trade follows the flag" is a long-recognized fact, of which the "Little England" faction would soon convince even its dullest adherents, were it to succeed in its unwisdom, and have hostile tariffs excluding British goods from Uganda and other vast

African regions, where it would fain see the Union Jack hauled down and foreign flags afloat.

Although, as will be seen in the following pages, a continuous chain of events has, during a series of years, been bringing into growing prominence the practical question of the organization of the Realms of Britain, probably never was its importance more conspicuously or—with complete absence of panic, it may be said—startlingly demonstrated than by the consideration of our naval position, which has occupied so much attention within the last few months. We are much indebted to one of our American kinsmen, Captain Mahan, for showing of what vital consequence to us—if we are to continue to exist as an Empire—the possession of sea power must be. No one could have rendered us a greater service; for the able and gallant writer, not being "a son and heir of the British Empire," has been able to state the question, as it affects us, with a calmness and impartiality which critics might try to gainsay, were he of our own nationality.

The recent discussions as to the state of the navy, have convinced the coolest and most hopeful of men, that the present possibilities of irreparable disaster to the Empire as a whole, and to all its component parts, great and small, should speedily be rendered impossible, by British naval supremacy being, once and for ever, placed beyond the chances of successful rivalry—as it well can be, by the matchless resources, strength, and positions which we can command, being utilized—as they ought to be, without delay—for the perfect defence of all our world-wide interests and dominions.

The defence of the Empire, being so all-important, requires to be dealt with by the very highest naval

and military authorities. One of them, Sir George S.
Clarke, has kindly written the chapter on "Imperial
Defence" for this work; and I have to thank him, as
I am sure all its readers will do, for his very valuable contribution, which will, doubtless, be of great
service to the cause, and will be most highly esteemed by those best acquainted with the question,
who know how thoroughly he has studied it, and how
ably he has always written about it. Many telling
quotations from Sir George Clarke might be inserted
here, giving timely warnings against " the doom which
awaits naval inferiority," and showing how effectually
it may be averted ; but the reader must have the
pleasure of perusing the chapter, without its freshness
being lost by the previous recital of any of its most
striking passages.

Iteration is either much to be condemned or much
to be commended. It cannot be too constantly repeated that Imperial Unity, as well as all our joint and
several interests—the Empire itself, and everything
within it—can only stand, just as every building does
on its foundations, upon British naval supremacy.
Once lost, that would be lost for ever—never to be
regained by any portion of that Empire, which would
be shattered by its destruction, except perhaps, some
centuries hence, by some British naval power which
might arise in Australia or South Africa. But this
supremacy—preserved, as it may well and easily be,
by a little united effort, at but light expense if fairly
divided—will be the joint property, the inalienable
heritage, the invaluable security of all Britons—without break from henceforth—as long as they have the
wisdom to remain in organized union.

The overthrow of the military power of France in

1870 was as nothing to her future, compared with what the consequences would be of the overthrow of British naval power—if smitten down in a maritime Sedan—to the Empire as a whole, to these Mother Isles of Britain, to the growth of the young Britains, of Canada, Australia, and South Africa, which might thus be crippled and deformed in their early years. British naval supremacy, so essential to all, should be maintained by all; for it is very doubtful if, with the increase and possible combinations of other navies, it will be worth anything like fifty years' purchase, if the Empire allow it to be much longer sustained, single-handed, by the brave little Mother Isles.

But we are not infrequently told that we already practically have British Federation—that nothing more is wanted, as we are so thoroughly united in sentiment. No doubt we are, and we should be most thankful for it. Sentiment, national affection, must be the basis of all political unity, and it is a strong and broad one upon which to build Imperial Federation. It should, however, never be forgotten that the most powerful sentiment, without efficient organization of material forces, never did, and never can, save nation or Empire from utter destruction by an enemy with weaker resources highly organized; and this must become more true in an age when success in war never so much depended upon weapons the most deadly and complicated, upon floating machines of Titanic force, upon scientific knowledge the most perfect and precise, and upon the skill, resource, and preparation of every man, from the highest in command to the humblest in our defensive services.

However inadequately I may have dealt with the momentous considerations pertaining to the great subject of which I have ventured to treat in this book, they lie at the very root of the question how the Empire, as a whole, and all its lands both great and small, can be placed in the best and strongest position for the fullest enjoyment of peace, security, and self-government, without panic or danger ever arising as regards general or individual safety.

With such vast common interests at stake, all that we require is suitable organization, which, backed by the force of strong existing sentiment, will render them invulnerable. Having for years availed myself of every opportunity of rendering any little help in my power, in urging the necessity for such organization, and in suggesting modes of obtaining it, I now, with the same object in view, venture to produce this work.

F. P. de LABILLIERE,

Harrow-on-the-Hill,
April, 1894.

CONTENTS.

CHAPTER I.

RISE OF THE FEDERAL PRINCIPLE.

CHAPTER II.

THE STARTING-POINT.

CHAPTER III.

PERMANENT UNITY OF THE EMPIRE.

CHAPTER IV.

MODES OF FEDERATION SUGGESTED.

CHAPTER V.

FIVE EXISTING FEDERATIONS.

CHAPTER VI.

POLITICAL ORGANIZATION OF THE EMPIRE.

CHAPTER VII.

IMPERIAL DEFENCE.

(By Major Sir George S. Clarke, R.E., K.C M.G.)

CHAPTER VIII.

THE CONTRACTION OF ENGLAND AND ITS ADVOCATES.

CHAPTER IX.

MARKING PROGRESS AND DEVELOPMENT.

CHAPTER X.

ESSENTIAL PRINCIPLES OF BRITISH FEDERATION.

CHAPTER XI.

LATER OBJECTIONS OF MR. GOLDWIN SMITH.

CHAPTER XII.

FRAMING A FEDERAL CONSTITUTION.

CHAPTER XIII.

A FEW CONCLUDING CONSIDERATIONS.

FEDERAL BRITAIN;

OR,

UNITY AND FEDERATION OF THE EMPIRE.

CHAPTER I.

RISE OF THE FEDERAL PRINCIPLE.

Governor Pownall on Consolidation of the Empire, in 1765—
Burke and Colonial Representation, in 1769—Adam Smith
regards difficulties as not "insurmountable," in 1776—Mr.
Robert Lowe on British Federalism, in 1844—Mr. Godley, in
1849 and 1852—Mr. Joseph Howe, in 1854—Mr. Edward
Blake, in 1874—Sir Julius Vogel, in 1877—Federal idea
revived in the Colonies—Honour of starting it divided—
"Australian Association" considers it in 1857—Earl Russell's
View in 1873—Paper Constitutions—Colonial Constitutions
and Canadian Federation rapidly take root—Great Power-
making capabilities of Federalism—Federation or separation
—American example—Drift and Disintegration advocated by
Professor Goldwin Smith and Lord Blachford—Opposition to
Policy of Incapacity aroused—Discussions at Bristol and
Cannon Street Meetings, in 1869—Imperial Federation: in
1871, at Conferences on Colonial Questions; in 1872, before
Social Science Congress at Devonport, in Mr. John Mathew's
book, and in speech of Lord Beaconsfield; in 1874, at
Glasgow; in 1875, 1881, and 1886 before Royal Colonial
Institute—Effect of opening of telegraph to Australia—Great
services of Royal Colonial Institute—Sir Frederick Young
and his "Imperial Federation"—Mr. Forster's address in
1875—Narrow Provincialists—Imperial Federation League—
Action of other Societies—The Imperial Institute—Change
in public opinion—Press and publications on question—
Colonial Conference of 1887—Two decades of growth.

WERE the inception and growth of the great idea
of developing the British Empire into a mighty

B

federation thoroughly investigated, the research would, probably, reveal the fact that many more men of thought and weight should be credited with holding the idea than are supposed to have ever entertained it.[1]

Few people on either side of the Atlantic, probably, ever contemplated the separation of the American Colonies from the Mother Country, till compelled to do so by the most unwise of policies. Before Lord North and George Grenville pressed their fatal measures, the principle of the permanent unity of the Empire would seem to have been universally taken for granted; but, doubtless, men of foresight gave thought to the question, how the position of the Colonies in the Empire could be improved by affording them a voice in its councils—an inquiry which, if followed up, must lead along the highway to Imperial Federation.

Perhaps the earliest writer to give expression— vaguely, no doubt—to the desire for organized permanent union[2] of the Empire was Governor Pownall, who had presided over three of the North American Colonies. In the dedication of his work to Grenville— a minister who was so soon to prove how inapplicable to himself the words would be—the author says:—

"May that minister who shall interweave the administration of the Colonies into the British administration, as a part essentially united with it, may he live to see the power, prosperity, and honour, that so great and important an event must give to

---

[1] With some additions and transpositions to other parts of this work, my paper, read before the Royal Colonial Institute on January 10, 1893, with the title of " British Federalism; Its Rise and Progress," forms this chapter.

[2] In his "Administration of the Colonies," 2nd edition, 1765. It is worth reading, to note how the old ideas of Colonial policy are the very opposite of those now so long, generally, received.

his country!" And at the outset the writer remarks that—
"The taking leading measures towards the forming all those
Atlantic and American possessions into one Empire, of which
Great Britain should be the commercial and political centre, is
the *precise duty* of Government at this crisis."

Had the men of his generation been prepared to
accept the new and wise teaching of Edmund Burke,
the unhappy rupture with the American Colonies
would never have taken place, and their relations with
the Mother Country would have become as amicable
as those with our present Colonies have been rendered,
by the policy originated by the great orator and statesman. On the principles enunciated by Burke is based
the present policy of maintaining the unity of our
race and Empire; and it was fitting that what is
most conducive to the future greatness of our British
nationality, both in its old and new dominions, should
have been set forth in the grandest eloquence of which
its language or any other is capable. The speeches[1]
which lay the foundation principles of our true
Imperial policy are imperishable, and we should hope
and strive that the national unity of our race may be
equally lasting.

All Burke's sympathies were in the direction of
British Federation, and doubtless, if he had had to deal
with the circumstances of our times, he would have
been an ardent Imperial Federalist. It has been said
that he even went as far as to have had some conference
or committee in Westminster, to consider the question
of Colonial representation in this country, or of
Federation; but to have come to the decision that the
policy was impracticable, by reason of the obstacles
interposed by distance and the slow means of com-

[1] "Conciliation with America," and "American Taxation."

munication, which then seemed incapable of improvement; and no wonder that such should have been the conclusion when steamers, railways, telegraphs, and telephones were unheard of.

In 1769 Burke pointed out the impossibility of the American Colonies being represented in the British Parliament, illustrating by the following vivid description the then existing difficulties:—

"The writs are issued for electing members for America and the West Indies. Some provinces receive them in six weeks, some in ten, some in twenty. A vessel may be lost, and then some provinces may not receive them at all. But let it be that they all receive them at once and in the shortest time. A proper space must be given for proclamation and for the election —some weeks at least. But the members are chosen, and if the ships are ready to sail, in about six more they arrive in London. In the mean time the Parliament has sat and business far advanced without American representatives. Nay, by this time it may happen that the Parliament is dissolved, and then the members ship themselves again to be again elected. The writs may arrive in America before the poor members of Parliament in which they never sat can arrive at their several provinces. A new interest is formed and they find other members are chosen whilst they are on the high seas. But if the writs and members arrive together, here is at best a new trial of skill amongst the candidates, after one set of them have well aired themselves with their two voyages of 6000 miles." [1]

No picture could present a more striking contrast between past circumstances, which seemed to render Imperial Federation impossible, and the present facilities for its realization. But we live in another century, and seem almost to be in another world, so vast have been the changes which have marvellously removed the impossibilities of the past.

[1] See Burke's "Observations on the State of the Nation," edition of his works published at Boston, i. 297.

Among the earliest believers in the possibility of contriving some system of federal organization for the Empire was certainly the famous Adam Smith, who pronounced as not "insurmountable" the difficulties of his day in the way of the representation of the Colonies in the English Parliament; for, seven years after the preceding extract from Burke was written, the great political economist expressed the following more hopeful opinion [1]:—

"There is not the least probability that the British Constitution would be hurt by the union of Great Britain and her Colonies. That constitution, on the contrary, would be completed by it, and seems to be imperfect without it. The assembly which deliberates and decides concerning the affairs of every part of the Empire, in order to be properly informed, ought certainly to have representatives from every part of it. That this union, however, could be easily effectuated, or that difficulties and great difficulties might not occur in the execution, I do not pretend. I have yet heard of none, however, which appear insurmountable. The principal, perhaps, arise, not from the nature of things, but from the prejudices and opinions of the people, both on this and on the other side of the Atlantic."

What a reflection it would be upon the lustre of the progress and enlightenment of the nineteenth or twentieth century should history have to record that, though the material difficulties of the eighteenth century had passed away, narrow prejudices, short-sighted provincial jealousies, or the selfish rivalries of traders or of politicians, alone remained "insurmountable" obstacles to the most beneficent policy of union and of Empire ever proposed to men of the same blood and language!

After the loss of the American Colonies, it must

[1] See "Wealth of Nations," published in 1776, Book IV. ch. vii.

have been difficult to imagine a federated Empire of
Great Britain, until the growth of her Australasian
and Canadian dominions brought the conception of
Imperial Federation into tangible shape, first as a
speculative and then as a practical question. The
earliest revival of the idea is, probably, that which I
unexpectedly discovered, in extracting materials for
my history of Victoria [1] from the New South Wales
Correspondence in the Record Office. There—in a
report of a debate in the Legislative Council at Sydney,
on August 20, 1844, when that, the first Australian
legislature in which the elective element appeared,
was only a year old—is a remarkable speech by Mr.
Robert Lowe, afterwards Lord Sherbrooke, on the
subject of the separation of the present Colony of
Victoria, in which he says :—

"As a general rule, he thought their (the Colonies) interests
were not consulted by frittering them away into minute particles,
but by combining as large a territory into a single state as
could be effectually controlled by a single Government. He
cordially agreed in the abstract truth of the motto prefixed
to the article in the newspaper of that morning, that "Union
is strength," and he would extend that principle to the whole
colonial empire of Great Britain. He hoped and believed that
the time was not remote when Great Britain would give up the
idea of treating the dependencies of the Crown as children, who
were to be cast adrift by their parent as soon as they arrived
at manhood, and substitute for it the far wiser and nobler policy
of knitting herself and her colonies into one mighty confederacy,
girdling the earth in its whole circumference and confident
against the world in arts and arms."

That eminent early New Zealand colonist, Mr. J.
R. Godley, gave powerful expression to his statesman-

[1] See ii. 274, and *Sydney Morning Herald*, Aug. 21, 1844.

like views respecting the maintenance of the unity of the Empire and on the subject of its federation. In a letter addressed to Mr. Gladstone from Plymouth, December 12, 1849, the day before leaving England, he says [1] :—

> " The best argument, perhaps, against separation is to be found in the strength and prevalence of a moral instinct which separatists do not recognize, and which they hardly understand, though they bear a strong testimony to its truth in the remarkable reluctance which they manifest to *avow* their doctrines. . . . I maintain that the love of empire, properly understood—that is, the instinct of self-development and expansion—is an unfailing symptom of lusty and vigorous life in a people; and that, subject to the conditions of justice and humanity, it is not only legitimate but most laudable. Certain am I that the decline of such a feeling is always the result not of matured wisdom or enlarged philanthropy, but of luxurious imbecility and selfish sloth. When the Roman eagles retreated across the Danube, not the loss of Dacia, but the satisfaction of the Roman people at the loss, was the omen of the empire's fall. Or, to take an illustration nearer home, it is unquestionable that, notwithstanding the disgraceful circumstances under which America was torn from the grasp of England, we suffered less in prestige and in strength by that obstinate and disastrous struggle than if, like the soft Triumvir, we had ' lost a world and been content to lose it.' Depend upon it, the instinct of national pride is sound and true."

No surer test than that of Mr. Godley could be invented to indicate whether, in our old or new dominions, individual Britons or British communities are up to the standard of the true metal, or are deteriorating from the high type of their race. The stamp is effaced, in proportion to the extent to which weakness may be discovered in " the instinct of national

---

[1] See his " Writings and Speeches," published in 1863, pp. 37, 123-4.

pride," or in " the love of empire;" for ours, above
all other empires, is surely worthy of the admiration
and affection of all its children and of their best
efforts to maintain its integrity and greatness; and
neither our " national pride " nor " love of empire "
requires the slightest surrender of that laudable patriotic
devotion due to our several dominions and provinces
from their respective sons, but only that they should
cultivate and cherish broadness of views and largeness
of sympathies.

In a lecture delivered in New Zealand, December 1,
1852, Mr. Godley mentions " the questions which it
would be right and proper to reserve from Colonial
jurisdiction, and place under the exclusive cognizance
of the Imperial Government;" and these he gives in
the words of Mr. Adderley, now Lord Norton :—

" First, the allegiance of the Colonies to her Majesty's Crown ;
2nd, the naturalization of aliens; 3rd, whatever relates to
treaties between the Crown and any foreign power; 4th, all
political intercourse and communications between any of the
Colonies and any officer of a foreign power; 5th, whatever relates to the employment, command and discipline of her
Majesty's troops and ships within the Colonies, and whatever
relates to the defence of the Colonies against foreign aggression,
including the command of the Colonial militia and marine in
time of war; and 6th, whatever relates to the crime of high
treason."

Then, a few lines further on, Mr. Godley thus
unmistakably declares for Imperial Federation :—

" Before the time arrives when these Colonies, conscious of
power, shall demand the privilege of standing on equal terms
with the Mother Country in the family of nations, I trust that
increased facility of intercourse may render it practical to
establish an Imperial Congress for the British Empire, in which

all its members may be fairly represented, and which may administer the affairs which are common to all."

Thus did the Federal idea begin to work in the Colonies, and its revival and wide extension was for the most part brought about by Colonial men. In 1854, that eminent Colonial-born statesman, Mr. Joseph Howe, spoke in the Legislature of Nova Scotia, powerfully advocating Imperial organization and defence. His speech [1] deserves to be carefully read; but here one or two gems from it must be extracted.

"Sir, I would not cling to England one single hour after I was convinced that the friendship of North America was under-valued, and that the status to which we may reasonably aspire has been deliberately refused. But I will endeavour, while asserting the rights of my native land with boldness, to per-petuate our connection with the British Isles, the home of our fathers, the cradle of our race.

＊　　＊　　＊　　＊　　＊　　＊

"The statesmen of England, Sir, may be assured, that if they would hold this great Empire together they must give the outlying portions of it some interest in the Naval, Military, and Civil Services, and I will co-operate with any man who will impress upon them the necessity for lengthening the ropes and strengthening the stakes, that the fabric which shelters us may not tumble about our ears.

＊　　＊　　＊　　＊　　＊　　＊

"Here, Sir, is work for the highest intellects; for the purest patriots on both sides of the Atlantic. Here is a subject worthy of the consideration of the largest-minded British statesmen now figuring on the stage of public life. . . . How insignificant are many of the topics which they debate in the Imperial Parliament compared with this. . . . How often I

[1] Published in London, by Ridgeway, in 1855, and his pamphlet, "The Organization of the Empire," in which he advocated Colonial representation in the Imperial Parliament, by Stanford, in 1855.

have said to myself, I wonder if it ever enters into the heads
of those noble Lords and erudite Commoners . . . that there
are two millions and a half of Christians in British America
who have no representative in either House. . . . I have often
thought, Sir, how powerful this Empire might be made; how
prosperous in peace, how invincible in war, if the statesmen
of England would set about its organization, and draw to a
common centre the high intellects which it contains.

"If the whole population were united by common interests,
no power on earth ever wielded means so vast, or influence so
irresistible. But, Sir, let the statesmen of England slumber
and sleep . . . while no provision is made to draw around the
Throne the hearts of millions predisposed to loyalty and
affection, and the result we may surely calculate."

In 1874,[1] Mr. Edward Blake, one of the most distinguished public men of Canada, and now a member
of the British House of Commons, thus advocated
Imperial Federation :—

"I took, three or four years ago, an opportunity of speaking,
and ventured to suggest that an effort should be made to re-
organize the Empire upon a Federal basis. I repeat what I
then said, that the time may be at hand when the people of
Canada shall be called upon to discuss the question. . . . The
Treaty of Washington produced . . . a feeling that at no distant
period the people of Canada would desire that they should
have some greater share of control than they now have in the
management of foreign affairs; that our Government should
not present the anomaly which it now presents—a Government
the freest, perhaps the most democratic in the world, with
reference to local and domestic matters, in which you rule
yourselves as fully as any people in the world, while in your
foreign affairs, your relations with other countries, whether
peaceful or warlike, commercial or financial, or otherwise, you
have no more voice than the people of Japan. This, however,

[1] In his speech at Aurora, on October 3rd, published at Ottawa,
with numerous comments from the Canadian press, in a pamphlet
entitled, "A National Sentiment."

is a state of things of which you have no right to complain,
because so long as you do not choose to undertake the responsibilities and burdens which attach to some share of control in
these affairs, you cannot fully claim the rights and privileges
of free-born Britons in such matters. . . . I believe, that while
it was not unnatural, not unreasonable, pending that process
of development which has been going on in our new and
sparsely settled country, that we should have been quite willing—we so few in numbers, so busied in our local concerns,
so engaged in subduing the earth and settling up the country—
to leave the cares and privileges to which I have referred in the
hands of the parent State; the time will come when that
national spirit which has been spoken of will be truly felt
among us, when we shall realize that we are four millions of
Britons who are not free, when we shall be ready to take up
that freedom, and to ask . . . our share of national rights.
To-morrow—by the policy of England, in which you have no
voice or control—this country might be plunged into the
horrors of a war. . . . That is a state of things of which you
will have no right to complain, as long as you can choose to say,
'We prefer to avoid the cares, the expenses and charges, and
we are unequal in point of ability to discharge the duties which
appertain to us as free-born Britons;' but while you say this,
you may not yet assume the lofty air, or speak in the high-
pitched tones which belong to a people wholly free."

Sir Julius Vogel, of New Zealand, also ably advocated the policy, an extract of what he wrote in 1877
being given at page 90.

The idea of British Federalism, as we have seen,
having, probably for the first time, been conceived
and evolved in the capacious intellect of Edmund
Burke, and regretfully abandoned by him in 1769 as
unattainable in the then condition of the world, and
having in 1776 been regarded by Adam Smith as a
speculative but possible policy, was revived by three
Colonists—in Australia, by Mr. Robert Lowe, in 1844;
in New Zealand, by Mr. Godley, in 1852; and in Canada,

by Mr. Joseph Howe, in 1854. These men—of large and statesmanlike views, of ample knowledge of the old country and of the Colonies, and looking at the question from such different standpoints—agreed in regarding some form of Imperial Federalism as desirable and practical, at a time when the Colonies were in such an infant stage of existence, and at such much greater distances from England and each other, by reason of duration of voyage and of the fact that neither steam, nor telegraphic communication, had been established, or seemed practicable, between our most widely separated dominions./ The honour, therefore, of starting the grand policy, though Colonists have the largest claim to it, must be shared, as it is desirable that it should be, and as the benefits of its realization will be, between Britons of the old and new lands of the Empire.

The efforts of "The General Association for the Australian Colonies," which existed in London from 1855 to 1862, in endeavouring to harmonize the relations of the Mother Country and Australia, ought not to be forgotten; and Mr. O'Halloran did well in contributing a sketch of its history to the *Colonies and India*, in 1884. It was founded with the principal object of promoting the passing of the Constitution Bills for the Australian Colonies, and at one time had as many as 231 members. Its hon. secretary and treasurer was Mr. (now Sir James) Youl, who recently presented the records of the Association to the Royal Colonial Institute. Among its leading members who ought to be mentioned, were Messrs. H. G. Ashurst, Captain C. H. Bagot, Niel Black, R. Brooks, W. Campbell, T. Chirnside, Hugh C. E. Childers, Sir Charles Clifford, Lord Alfred Churchill, F. G. Dalgety, F. A.

Du Croz, F. H. Dutton, W. F. de Salis, Sir Stuart A. Donaldson, A. L. Elder, J. Hawdon, Arthur Hodgson, D. Larnach, T. Learmouth, Sir William McArthur, Lachlan Mackinnon, Sir George MacLeay, J. Morrison, Sir Charles Nicholson, W. Rutledge, E. Stephens, Alderman Salamons, W. C. Wentworth, W. Westgarth, and Edward Wilson. Most of them are now gone, but happily several of them are with us still. The Australian Association dealt with Intercolonial Federation, and representation of the Colonies in this country did not escape its consideration. In 1855, when the Australian constitutions were under discussion, it presented a memorial to Lord John Russell, then Secretary for the Colonies, setting forth that "the Constitutions of the Colonies forming the Australian group will be incomplete until a Federal Assembly is constituted." The Government, however, declined to entertain the proposal until the Colonial legislatures should express a desire on the subject. Next year the Association addressed Mr. Labouchere, afterwards Lord Taunton, who had become Secretary for the Colonies, upon "The necessity of Parliament passing a Permissive Bill empowering the Australian Colonies to form a Federal Assembly." It also presented a draft bill with the memorial, but no action was taken by the Government. In 1857, a special general meeting of the members of the Association dealt with the following proposal, which involved the principle of Imperial Federation :—

"That a memorial be presented by the Association to the Secretary of State for the Colonies, requesting that he will be pleased, in the Cabinet deliberations on the forthcoming Reform Bill, to represent to her Majesty's Ministers the strong claims of the Colonies to some share of representation in the Imperial

Legislature, but that it be at the same time expressed to Mr. Labouchere that, in the opinion of this Association, the Colonies could not accept of Parliamentary representation unless their present rights of self-taxation be continued and preserved to them inviolate."

After consideration by the meeting, the motion was withdrawn, as it was regarded as inopportune. The Australian Association also did valuable work in promoting steam communication with the Colonies, in obtaining more adequate naval defence, and the establishment of a Commodore's station in the Australian waters, in getting the sovereign admitted as a legal tender, and in the introduction of salmon to the rivers of Tasmania, to which Sir James Youl specially and laboriously devoted himself. The utility of such an Association was undoubted, at a time when the Colonies had not advanced to the stage of having official representatives in this country.

It is more than probable that that eminent statesman, Earl Russell, had formed decided views on Britannic Federalism long before giving expression to them in his "Recollections and Suggestions," from 1813–1873, in which he says:—

"I am disposed to believe that if a Congress or Assembly representing Great Britain and her dependencies could be convoked from time to time, to sit for some months in the autumn, arrangements reciprocally beneficial might be made. . . . In my eyes it would be a sad spectacle—it would be a spectacle for gods and men to weep at—to see this brilliant Empire, the guiding star of freedom, broken up—to behold Nova Scotia, the Cape of Good Hope, Jamaica, and New Zealand try each its little spasm of independence; while France, the United States, and Russia would be looking at each, willing to annex one or more fragments to the nearest part of their dominions."

The foregoing instances suffice to show that the Federal idea was not lost sight of by practical and far-seeing statesmen, even before it had to any extent attracted the attention of political theorists, or even reached the first stage of consideration, so well described by the writer quoted in Sir Frederick Young's " Imperial Federation," p. 134, who says :—

" The law of political as of all progress seems to me to be this : first, we hear a few whispers in the cabinet of the student; then the question passes into the area of scientific inquiry; finally, after long maturing, after a severe and searching controversy, it enters the sphere of actual truth, and moulds human action."

The Colonies, however, were rapidly passing out of their infant years. Their marvellous growth had eclipsed all experience or expectation. They had to be speedily equipped with the institutions of self-government. These could only be supplied by paper constitutions—the aversion of some sticklers for precedent—for the need of Colonial organization would not permit that the governmental systems of the Colonies should be evolved through long ages, like the grand old model, British Constitution, from which all the free and good governments of the world have, directly or indirectly, been derived. As the Colonies could not wait for institutions of slow growth, neither can they, nor the Empire at large, postpone, for anything like half a century, the inauguration of some federal system, if our Imperial union is to be rendered effective and all-powerful to safeguard our vast and growing common interests on land and sea.

Besides the Republic of the United States, the Empires of Germany and Austria-Hungary have, during the last two decades, been furnishing to the

world striking examples of the great power-making
capabilities of federalism, even when contending with
difficulties and drawbacks more serious than those
arising out of the circumstances of our widespread
Empire.   The remarkable rise and growth of the
federal constitution of Canada—a mere paper constitution, as were all those of the Colonies not many
years back—is by itself an object lesson for the people
of the Empire, sufficient to instruct them in the
advantages of federation.   The Dominion Act—that
paper constitution only a quarter of a century ago—
a veritable slip, full of vitality, of the old British
Constitution, no sooner touched the soil of Canada
than, like a tropical tree in a congenial clime, it at
once struck down its roots and sent up its foliage, and,
like the hardiest giant of the forest amid the snows
of a North American winter, it already seems to stand
as firm as the ancient, slowly-developed constitution
of the parent land.

It would have been extraordinary if, after the establishment of provincial self-government in Australia,
and of Intercolonial Federation in Canada, thoughtful
men had not soon begun to consider what further
developments would be needed, to complete the political
organization of our United Empire; and a little
reflection would soon bring home the conviction that
one of two things is ultimately inevitable—Federation
or Separation.   In either we must follow the example
of our kinsmen of the United States; and why should
the alternative for us be that most undesirable one,
which the foolish policy of last century—the reverse
of our present Colonial policy—forced upon the
Americans?   Some illogical people take the unhappy
historical fact that the United States were driven into

independence, as a conclusive reason why the present British Colonies must sooner or later go out of the Empire. Let us follow our American kinsmen, not in the paths of separation, into which they most unwillingly entered, but in the great example they have given the world, of how a number of States may retain all the advantages of complete provincial self-government in combination with those of national unity; and may thus secure a position among the greatest Powers on earth, by means of the easy bond of well-organized federation. When an American like Mr. Henry George [1] tells us that the United States might even now not be independent, but for the attempt "to crush the American Colonies into submission"—which he says had "the effect of splitting into two what might but for that have perhaps yet been one great confederated nation"—surely none but a few short-sighted, faint-hearted, or cross-grained Britishers can be found, in any part of our United Empire, to believe that there must ever be any necessity for its dismemberment.

With the conviction that the maturity of the Colonies must bring change in their relations to each other and to the Mother Country, no clear policy was, at first, presented, save in such isolated instances as have been already mentioned. For a time there seemed to be a general feeling that things must be allowed to drift. In this stage of stagnation sprang up that noxious negation of a policy, the idea of disintegration. This was boldly, and, no doubt, ably, advocated by Professor Goldwin Smith in a series of letters, published in the *Daily News*, in 1862–63, and, in the latter year, in a volume called "The Empire."

[1] "Social Problems," chap. xvi.

The title is defective, the words, " And how to get rid
of it," being required to complete it; for such was the
tenour of the work.   The clear and simple course of
letting the Empire fall to pieces, which requires no
energy, statesmanship, or ability, had an attraction for
some minds at a time when no decided Imperial policy
was in prospect.   To prepare the Colonies for being
cast adrift, or for "self-reliance"—Mr. Smith's expression to soften the idea—was the policy of Sir
Frederick Rogers, the permanent head of the Colonial
Office, who for eleven years had the ear of several of
its political chiefs.   On retiring with a peerage as
Lord Blachford, he contributed, in 1877, to the
Nineteenth Century Review, an article decidedly favourable to disintegration.   How much wider and wiser
have been the views of his successor, Sir Robert
Herbert, who has also recently retired from the office!
    It was not to be supposed that men of British blood
and spirit—of the race having "the genius of universal
empire," as the American orator, Mr. Depew, has
well described it—would long leave in undisputed
possession of the field a policy of incapacity, which
hopelessly proclaimed that all the splendid materials
for Empire-building—which the genius and energy of
our race were accumulating—should be left helplessly
to drift, instead of being fitted together into the
grandest Imperial structure it is possible for the
world to behold.   The suggestion of disruption, made
by a few persons, was speedily answered by many
voices raising the patriotic cries of " United Empire,"
"Permanent Unity," which have ever since echoed
and re-echoed in every British land.
    The opposition called forth by the public advocacy
of disintegration, at first confined itself to directing

the attention of both Mother Country and Colonies to the value to them of their union. It was only to be expected that men best acquainted with the latter should have most clearly seen, and decidedly declared, the truth as to this point, at a time when it was not so conspicuous as the development of the Colonial Empire has since made it. A large and influential number of Colonists attended the Social Science Congress at Bristol in September, 1869, when the question of the relations of England and the Colonies was discussed, papers being read by Mr. (now Sir John) Gorst, Mr. Thomas Hare, myself,[1] and Mr. John Noble, all but the last being favourable to the unity of the Empire; but its federation, if barely alluded to, was not advocated. Among speakers of weight who took part in the discussion were Sir William Denison and Mr. Edward Wilson.

The latter gentleman, being strongly impressed with the conviction that an important point had been reached in Colonial progress, took steps for calling together the Cannon Street meetings, which had no little share in giving a right direction to the current of opinion. They were held at the large station hotel, and, beginning at the end of November, 1869, took place weekly for five or six weeks. The chair was ably filled by Sir James A. Youl. The object of these meetings was to call attention to the advantages of the unity of the Empire, and to indicate points upon which its relations might be improved; but all of us who were present were, no doubt, still only groping our way to a practical policy of organized union, to place in opposition to the destructive proposals of the Disruptionists. The Cannon Street meetings mark the rise of a better

[1] See page 36.

feeling as regards Mother Country and Colonies, and they left on record, among others, two valuable resolutions, both drawn by a good friend of the cause, the late Mr. William Westgarth. The first, moved by him, affirmed "That the Colonies are the source of great commercial, political, and social advantages to the parent country, and largely contribute to the influence and greatness of the Empire."

As it was thought that the mover of the second resolution, affirming the benefits to the Colonies of the Imperial connection, should be of Colonial birth, I had the honour of being called on to propose—

"That, on the other hand, the rights of Imperial citizenship, Imperial supervision, influence, and example, and Imperial commerce and resources, promote all the best interests of the Colonies, and they on their part are not wanting in a loyal appreciation of their beneficial relationship."

The idea of Imperial Federation was not broached at the Cannon Street meetings; and this is not to be wondered at, seeing that, in 1869, a telegraphic cable had not been carried to Australia, the opening of the Canadian Pacific Railway was a prospect in the dim distance, and the speedy development of our present highly improved means of communication was so little anticipated. For a time nothing more worthy of the Empire than a mere council of advice was suggested; but in the January number of the *Contemporary Review* for 1871, appeared an article headed, "Imperial Federation," by Mr. Edward Jenkins, proposing a Federal Parliament for Imperial affairs, indicating the questions with which it should deal, and showing that provincial concerns should be left to provincial governments. Mr. Jenkins also pointed out that, in the previous session of what is called the Imperial Parliament, only 48 Acts, out of 293 passed, were really Imperial.[1]

On July 20, 1871, at the Conference on Colonial questions,[2] to which I was honorary secretary, held at the Westminster Palace Hotel, I read a paper on "Imperial and Colonial Federalism,"[3] in which I advocated an Imperial Federal Parliament and Executive; and in the discussion following, which, I believe, was the first public one on the subject ot Imperial Federation, that policy was supported by Mr. Jenkins, Mr. J. Dennistoun Wood, and Sir Frederick Young, whilst Mr. Edward Wilson, though sympathetic, did not think the scheme practical.

Next year (1872) Mr. Jehu Mathews, of Toronto, brought out his valuable work in favour of Imperial Federation, treating the subject with considerable detail; and, in October, Mr. Jenkins and I again brought forward the question, by reading papers before the Social Science Congress at Devonport. In December, there appeared in *Frazer's Magazine* an article powerfully supporting the policy, entitled, "Empire or no Empire." It was dated "Melbourne, August, 1872," bore the initials "W. J. S.," and stated that the writer was a Colonist of twenty years' standing.

A remarkable pronouncement in favour of British Federalism, also made in 1872, was that of the famous Lord Beaconsfield, at the Crystal Palace, on June 24, when he said—

[1] In the longest of sessions, that of 1893, the vital question of the Naval defence of the Empire could not be dealt with in proper time; Irish Home Rule, Parish Councils, Employers' Liabilities—measures, however wise or unwise, relating to the provincial affairs of the British Isles—stopping the way of all Imperial questions.

[2] The proceedings were published in a volume entitled, "Discussions on Colonial Questions."

[3] See page 61.

"I cannot conceive how our distant Colonies can have their affairs administered except by self-government. But self-government, in my opinion, when it was conceded, ought to have been conceded as part of a great policy of Imperial consolidation. . . . It ought, further, to have been accompanied by the institution of some representative Council in the metropolis, which would have brought the Colonies into constant and continuous relations with the Home Government. . . . In my opinion, no Minister in this country will do his duty who neglects any opportunity of reconstructing, as much as possible, our Colonial Empire, and of responding to those distant sympathies which may become the source of incalculable strength and happiness to this land."

The opening of telegraphic communication with Australia had a powerful effect upon the question. It proved that the remotest dominions of the United Empire, are in more immediate contact with its metropolis, than were the most distant parts of the United Kingdom in the early years of this century. At the banquet of November 13, 1872, to celebrate the event, to a telegram despatched as the guests sat down a reply from the other side of the globe was within two hours read by the chairman. The toast, "The Integrity of the British Empire," given, perhaps, for the first time, "was received with immense enthusiasm and cries of 'Hurrah!' that lasted for several minutes."[1] I never witnessed anything more impressive than that great gathering of men from all parts of the Empire, springing to their feet and acclaiming their devotion to its unity.

In October, 1874, Mr. C. W. Eddy brought the question of the relations of the Colonies to the Empire again under discussion, at the Glasgow meeting of the

[1] See report of the banquet, *Proceedings of the Royal Colonial Institute*, vol. iii.

Social Science Congress, immediately before his sudden death; and his paper was afterwards also read at the Royal Colonial Institute, of which he had been honorary secretary. At the beginning of 1875, this Society occupied two meetings in discussing Imperial Federation, the question being opened by me with a paper entitled, "The Permanent Unity of the Empire."[1]

Subsequently, Imperial Federation has been frequently before the Institute, either as the subject of papers read at its meetings or incidentally in its discussions. I again had the honour of twice introducing it, in 1881 by a paper on "The Political Organization of the Empire," and also at the Conference held under the auspices of the Institute at the Colonial Exhibition, South Kensington, in 1886, by a paper entitled, "Imperial Federation."[2]

Many incidents worthy of notice in the development of the great policy may escape observation, but no greater oversight could be committed than to fail to observe, how the rise of the unity and federal principles and of the Royal Colonial Institute, have been contemporaneous, and have doubtless helped each other. Founded in 1868, on the suggestion of Mr. A. R. Roche, its first honorary secretary, and with Lord Bury, now Earl of Albemarle, as its virtual founder and first President, it was not long before the Institute was seen to be supplying a great want.

---

[1] Reproduced in Chapter III.

[2] These papers are reproduced at pages 86, 186. Besides the discussion of Imperial Unity and Federation above referred to, and incidental mention of them in connection with other subjects brought before the Royal Colonial Institute, in twenty-two volumes of its *Proceedings*, are twenty-seven papers bearing on the question.

There had been previous attempts to create centres of Colonial interest in the metropolis of the Empire, such as the Australian Association already spoken of, and the rooms started by it, which for a short time existed at the Jerusalem Coffee House, Cornhill; but for breadth of interests, largeness of sympathies, and comprehensiveness of objects, nothing like this Institute had ever been designed. It was early evident that much more than had been sought for had been found; that the new Society possessed those possibilities of development which have been so largely realized—that not merely a club or social meeting-place—agreeable as the Institute has in this way become—had been founded, but a great national institution with a noble principle, expressed in the two words of its motto, "United Empire," and with a great work which has year by year been expanding during two decades and a half. In all truth and fairness, it must be acknowledged that some of the strongest and happiest influences, in promoting the best relations between all parts of the Empire, have been exercised by the Institute and by its Resident and Non-Resident Fellows—numbering now almost four thousand—who, collectively and individually, have been heartily promoting the good cause of unity in every British land. There can be no doubt about this if we attempt to estimate the amount of good done by the Royal Colonial Institute, in bringing together men from all parts of the Empire, in promoting the feelings of nationality and brotherhood among them, in increasing their knowledge of each other as well as of their respective countries, and in cultivating among them the idea of permanent unity and federation. The toast of "The Queen and United

Empire," always given at its dinners, the simple device of Union Jacks and trident as its badge, with the motto, "United Empire," sent forth on tens of thousands of letters and papers to every corner of our dominions, have all contributed to the growth of the grand idea, and so has the annual volume of the *Proceedings*, distributed by thousands far and wide throughout Britain within and beyond these seas. I feel it is not unbecoming in any member of the Institute, to speak so strongly of what it has done and is doing, because I know I am saying no more than the exact truth.

The late Duke of Manchester, who in the early and uphill days of the Institute took such an active part in its affairs, and seldom failed to preside at its meetings, was ever ready to avail himself of opportunities of commending Imperial Federation at a time when its advocates were but few.

Mr. S. W. Silver, a warm supporter of the good cause, lent the *Colonies* newspaper, which he founded, to its advocacy; and for two or three years, about twenty years ago, its articles, written by Professor Bonamy Price, and by myself, strongly advocated the unity of the Empire, mine being decidedly in favour of Imperial Federation. At the end of 1875, a correspondence was opened in this journal by Sir Frederick Young, who had for an opponent a writer with the signature "Colonus." Others also joined in; and, on the close of the discussion, Sir Frederick reproduced the correspondence, as well as other contributions upon the subject, in his valuable work, "Imperial Federation." He has, from the beginning of the great revival of the federal principle, been an able advocate and zealous apostle of the good cause. From the time of the Cannon Street meetings, where I had the pleasure of making his acquaintance, he has taken part in most discussions of the question.

A powerful impetus was, undoubtedly, given to the principle of maintaining the unity of the Empire and to Imperial Federation, by the address on " Our Colonial Empire," delivered in Edinburgh, on November 5, 1875, by the Right Hon. W. E. Forster. It was felt that any cause taken up by this distinguished statesman, who was so universally trusted and so eminently practical, could be no longer regarded as a mere dream or speculation. Mr. Forster not only adduced very strong arguments in support of the principle of unity, but clearly pointed to Imperial Federation as the means of preserving it.

"Surely [he said] it cannot be denied that, if it be possible to replace dependence by association, each member of the federation would find in the common nationality at least as much scope for its aspirations, as much demand for the patriotism, and the energy, and the self-reliance of its citizens, as it would if trying to obtain a distinct nationality of itself."

And further on are these words of wisdom :—

" All that is required now is to imbue them—the Colonies— and ourselves with the desire that the Union should last, with the determination that the Empire should not be broken up— to replace the idea of eventual independence, which means disunion, by that of association on equal terms, which means union. If this be done, we need not fear that at the fitting time this last idea will realize itself."

Mr. Forster, in dealing with Imperial Federation, was able to affirm that which, if Burke could have said, he would not have felt constrained to abandon the policy :—

" Science has brought together the ends of the earth and made it possible for a nation to have oceans roll between its provinces. Why, then, should we alone among the nations set ourselves against that desire for nationality which is one of the most powerful ideas of the age ? What right have we to entail upon the men of our race the dangers and disadvantages of disunion ? Why should we reject the gifts of science, and neglect the possibilities of union which steam and electricity afford? . . . May not we and our Colonists together, by the exercise of some mutual forbearance, by willingness to incur some mutual sacrifice, hope to transform our Colonial Empire into a federation of peaceful, industrious, law-abiding commonwealths, so that in due time our British brotherhood may prove to the world, as no nation has ever proved before, 'How good and how pleasant it is for brethren to dwell together in unity.' "

Thus was the policy of Imperial Federation developed out of the aspiration of the people of the Empire for the permanence of their unity; and, as it advanced, that inane substitute for a policy, drift and disintegration—so unworthy of our Imperial race—receded before it, to retain as supporters only a few doctrinaires and narrow provincialists, who are too short-sighted to perceive, that the surest guarantees for the fullest local developments and self-government, are to be found in the strength and security of Imperial unity, rather than in complete provincial independence.

In his " Australian Federation,"[1] Mr. Howard Willoughby says : " The provincialist will, of course, never be won over to any scheme," and that it is " his small-minded and selfish idea that you benefit a locality by isolating it from its national whole ; " but, adds the writer, " happily for mankind, more generous impulses and truer instincts—those that tell us that

[1] Published in Melbourne, in 1891.

all men's good is each man's benefit—are in the end usually triumphant."

The next step forward was the formation of the League for the special advocacy of Imperial Federation. It was evident, when the principle of maintaining the unity of the Empire had been so widely accepted, and the idea of its federal union adopted by so many people, that the time had arrived for a further advance. Accordingly, early in 1884, in a conversation with Sir John Colomb, I suggested the formation of a society with the special object of promoting the policy of Imperial Federation; and we determined to seek the co-operation of some whose sympathies we knew to be warmest in the cause. The result was that a small committee was formed consisting of, besides ourselves, Sir George Baden-Powell, the late Mr. William Westgarth, Mr. J. Dennistoun Wood, and Sir Frederick Young.

After some deliberations, the members of the committee, except Sir George Baden-Powell and Mr. Westgarth, who were unable to attend its meetings, had an interview, on April 9, 1884, with Mr. Forster, to whom they submitted a proposal that he and other public men should be invited to a conference which should be strictly non-party in its composition; and that those consenting to attend, should do so on the understanding that they accepted the principle, that the unity of the Empire ought to be permanently maintained. Mr. Forster declared himself decidedly favourable to the conference being held on the basis proposed, and granted permission to the committee to mention him as being willing to take part in it.

Having succeeded in securing for the movement

the inestimable advantage of having such a statesman at its head, the Provisional Committee added to its numbers Mr. H. O. Arnold-Forster, Sir Daniel Cooper, Bart. (New South Wales), Messrs. W. J. Courthope, R. R. Dobell (Canada), William Gisborne (New Zealand), Hon. Harold Finch-Hatton, Alex. Staveley Hill, Q.C., M.P., Sir Roper Lethbridge, J. B. Watt (New South Wales), and Sir Samuel Wilson (Victoria). The committee, which by the permission of the Council held all its meetings at the old rooms of the Royal Colonial Institute in the Strand, lost no time in making the arrangements for the conference, which took place at the Westminster Palace Hotel on July 29, 1884, under the presidency of Mr. Forster. It affirmed the principle that, " to secure the permanent unity of the Empire, some form of Federation is essential," and also resolved that " a society be formed of men of all parties, to advocate and support the principle of federation." The first resolution was moved by the Right Hon. W. H. Smith, M.P., and seconded by the Earl of Rosebery, and the second by Mr. Edward Stanhope, M.P., and seconded by Mr. Mowat, Premier of Ontario.

The Provisional Committee—of which up to this time I was honorary secretary, and afterwards jointly with Mr. Arnold-Forster—was empowered to arrange the details of the organization of the new Society, and to report to an adjourned meeting of the conference, which was held on November 18, 1884. Mr. Forster, who had given much time and consideration to the preparations of the committee, was again in the chair. On this occasion the Imperial Federation League was formally established, the motion for its foundation being proposed by the late Marquis of Normanby,

seconded by the present Lord Knutsford, and supported by Mr. Edward Stanhope. The second resolution, appointing the first General Committee to conduct
the affairs of the League, was moved by the Premier
of Canada, Sir John A. Macdonald—that great Colonial
statesman, who, as Lord Rosebery has so well said,
"had grasped the central idea that the British Empire
is the greatest secular agency for good now known to
mankind." Sir William Fox, ex-Premier of New
Zealand, seconded the proposal.

The League continued the advocacy of the great
policy, first under the presidency of Mr. Forster, and
after his lamented death, of another distinguished
statesman, Lord Rosebery, who, on accepting the office
of Secretary of State for Foreign Affairs in Mr. Gladstone's Government, was succeeded by Mr. Stanhope—
Secretary for War in the previous Ministry—whose
death, at the end of 1893, was a loss to the Empire.
He was one of the most perfect models of an English
gentleman; and will be remembered as the Minister
who summoned the first Colonial Conference, in 1887.
The League established many branches in this country,
a very strong one in Canada, and some in Australia.
It circulated a large amount of literature upon the
subject, and by public meetings and lectures did much
to familiarize the public mind of the Empire with the
question. Its monthly journal, *Imperial Federation,*
was of great service in promoting the cause.

It is to be regretted that the rather sudden demise
of the League must now be recorded; for, at a
meeting of its Council, on November 24, 1893, it
was resolved "that the central organization be dissolved at the close of the present year;" and after
an attempt to keep the journal alive, it has also

ceased to exist. Further on,[1] in its proper place, the expediency of the course taken will be considered; but it may be here accounted for by the fact that the expenses of the society from the first were known to be borne by a few rich, generous supporters; so that sufficient importance was not attached to the enrolment of a large number of annual subscribers of small sums —a matter which would have had due attention, had the executive sought to build up the organization of the League by steps, instead of launching out into office expenses far beyond its income from ordinary subscribers.

The formation of the United Empire Trade League was proof of the growth of the interest taken in Imperial questions; and the object of harmonizing, as far as possible, our tariffs and commercial systems, must command the sympathies of all Imperial Unionists, however they may regard the ends of the League as attainable. The success of Mr. Henniker Heaton, in cheapening and improving Imperial postage, also shows the right flow of a true policy.

Among bodies in this country whose discussions have materially aided the cause of Imperial unity and organization are the Society of Arts, the United Service Institution, and the London Chamber of Commerce. In fact, our great policy is sure to have an important bearing upon some of the subjects within the scope of most societies with a broad platform. It is to be hoped that the new Imperial Institute will do much to foster the unity and federal feeling. The rise of such a great organization furnishes powerful proof of the growth of the United Empire policy.

The great change in public opinion regarding

[1] Page 223.

extensions of the Empire affords striking proof of the
strength attained by a healthy and enlightened Imperial national feeling. The movement, started about
the time of the Cannon Street meetings, and vigorously
promoted by the Royal Colonial Institute, soon sunk
the policy of curtailing the Empire which had got
afloat; but the mischievous idea, held even by some
good friends of Imperial unity, that the Empire was
large enough, and ought not to be extended, was
harder to kill. It lived long enough to lose for us
half, and nearly the whole, of eastern New Guinea,
which the Imperial Government, had it acted upon
the repeated representations of the Council of the
Royal Colonial Institute, would have annexed in good
time.[1] The survival to any influential extent of this
idea, would for ever have politically excluded us from
those grand regions in South and Central Africa, which
are being just brought under that flag of ours, without
which our trade could never enter; for the Powers
which would be quick to appropriate any magnificent
piece of Empire, were we foolish enough to throw it
away, would effectually keep out our commerce by
high protective tariffs. Some "Little Englanders"
thought the time, when the cruel rule of the Matabele
savages was being so well put down, as most fitting
to attempt the revival of the small policy of Imperial
contraction. To hold and develop the splendid new
territory to their north, merely with a view to their
own best advantage, South Africans, whether of British

[1] The first New Guinea Blue Book, laid before Parliament in
1876, contains the report of a deputation on the subject, from the
Institute to the Colonial Office in 1875; also my letter to Lord
Carnarvon in 1874, advocating annexation, a copy of which was sent
with a covering despatch to the Governors of all the Australian
Colonies.

or Dutch origin, must see that the strength of an Imperial organization will be all-important, and that they must never think of standing alone among so many great Powers who will be their neighbours. The finest position for the most commanding naval station of the world is in South Africa. All the great maritime Powers may well covet it, and, were she independent, might contend for it. The Afrikander can only confidently assure himself of its possession by well-organized federal union with the Empire.

The support which, for some years, the press throughout the Empire has, so largely, given to British unity and federalism, is conclusive evidence of the growth of the great policy. To mention some journals would be invidious; a complete list would be too long to be given. Some idea of the amount of what has been written on the question may be formed by looking through Mr. Boosé's "Titles of Publications in Connection with Imperial Policy." One of the most important, which had a very great influence on the question, is Professor Seeley's standard work, the "Expansion of England."

The rise of the policy of Britannic Federalism was marked in a notable manner by the meeting in London of the Colonial Conference of 1887, in which all the self-governing provinces of the Empire were represented. It was a great object lesson in Imperial Federation, though the question itself was excluded from discussion. The creation of the Australian naval squadron was an important federal arrangement; and the conference itself was undoubtedly a federal assembly, though of a very elementary description. The periodical meetings of such a body would be actual federation in the first stage of development.

During the two decades since the revival of British Federalism that policy has been steadily advancing, at one time slowly, at another with leaps and bounds. At present its progress is, perhaps, not so visible; but the germination of newly-sown seed in the best of soils is not at once apparent, and plants, when striking down their first and strongest roots, often make least promise of future growth. The cause has outstripped the expectations of the most hopeful of its early advocates. These practical promoters of a practical policy, though ready themselves to go at a quicker pace, may be well content when they see public opinion flowing in the right direction. As long as it is set that way it would be injudicious, by attempting to put on high-pressure speed, to alarm many people who prefer to be carried more slowly along.

CHAPTER II.

THE STARTING-POINT.

Process of arriving at belief in Federation—Idea of Intercolonial leads up to Imperial Federation—Britons should deprecate any suggestion of separation—Advantage to Britons of not becoming foreigners to each other—Defence of Colonies at different stages of their growth—Feeling the way towards organized unity—A splendid vision—England nursing infant nations—Unity in Empire their grandest future.

HAVING noted the fact of the rise and expansion of the Federal principle, we shall perceive, as we advance, the mental process by which the idea is evolved; we shall trace the development, out of the patriotic aspiration for the permanent political unity of our race, of the practical policy of its Federation. The two are very closely related, as cause and effect. A strong conviction that the Empire is one, and should be rendered indivisible, must be the starting-point—the source, so to speak, of the stream, so that if a man embark upon it he must smoothly glide down to the inevitable landing-place. He cannot long remain stationary in the current. Unless of a peculiar mental constitution, he must, if he continue thinking, arrive at the conclusion that some federal system will ultimately be indispensable. His ideas may be crude, he may protest that he can never see his way to Federation —that he does not believe in anything more than the occasional meeting of a Colonial Conference, or, at the most, the formation of some kind of permanent Council of advisers for the Empire. If he go so far, the federal idea is dawning upon him.

If I may venture to state the process by which I arrived at Imperial Federation—or British Federalism, as some may prefer it called—I believe that most of my readers who have thought out the question, will find they came to that conclusion in similar ways; along which others may be led by those who have already travelled by them. As a youth in Australia, I was first attracted to Intercolonial Federation by thinking of what it might do for my native land. Then the horizon of my views gradually expanded, so as to enable me to see the advantages Imperial Federation would bring to her, as well as to every other British land, including the Mother Isles of the Empire. In my earliest attempt to deal with the question of " The Future Relations of England and her Colonies,"[1] in 1869, I did not think of suggesting Federation. The States of Younger Britain seemed then in a stage of infancy too early for such a policy to be considered, except as a remote speculation. I therefore confined myself to argue against disintegration, and to point out the advantages, to all concerned, of maintaining the union—the chief reasons for which need not be repeated here, as they were again more fully urged in my paper before the Royal Colonial Institute, in 1875, reproduced in the next chapter. To preserve, however, the thread of the discussion from the first, only a few observations from my Bristol paper require to be quoted.

[1] In a paper with that title read before the Social Science Congress at Bristol, and published in its *Transactions.*

Speaking, then, on September 30, 1869, as one born in Melbourne and brought up in Australia, I said that the idea of dismembering the British Empire should never be entertained by any good Old Country, or Colonial, Englishman; that any suggestion of separation could not be too severely censured; that no man not meaning to make mischief, between England and the Colonies, should begin the solution of difficulties by talking of separation, or of the interruption of good relations; and that it is clearly an advantage that Britons in these Isles and Britons and their sons in the Colonies, should never be foreigners to each other. I contended that existing questions between Mother Country and Colonies could be easily adjusted; and, that as to defence, the general principle might be laid down—that neither should England tax the Colonies, nor should they tax her. Whatever was to be the rule with regard to defence, should be impartially carried out with respect to all colonies similarly circumstanced; though there may be two or three classes of colonies which should be differently treated. It may be difficult to draw a practical distinction; but, as a matter of fact, a nation with numerous colonies must exercise towards them different degrees of care. There will be the helpless infant colony, which cannot subsist without maternal protection; the half-grown colony, not yet equal to bear the whole expense of its own defence; and the colony sufficiently advanced to pay for its fortifications, and to keep up a militia or volunteer force.[1] The Australian Colonies are examples of the last class. They have for years borne the expense of their harbour defences, and have maintained an effective force of volunteers. There is little doubt that,

[1] See page 175.

should Australia remain united to England, as there is every hope she may, when her population is five, ten, twenty millions or more, she will consider it a point of honour to contribute towards the general defence of the Empire.[1] If both she and England desire to remain in partnership, it will be easy to arrange that Australia shall keep up a squadron, incorporated with the Imperial navy, for the defence of the Empire in the Southern waters. About twenty years after it was made, this suggestion was carried out.

In regard to organized unity, I was still, like everyone else twenty-five years ago, only feeling my way towards such a thing. The most I could say was in the following concluding paragraphs of my paper :—

" What I hope for in the future is an Australian Confederation, a Canadian Confederation, a South African Confederation, in union with Old England, either with or without representation in her Parliament; all cheerfully taking part in maintaining the power of the Empire. ' Union is strength.' As the Colonies grow and strengthen, each will be stronger for such a union; the Mother Country will feel it a support, and both she and the Colonies will be at far less expense for defences, if all stand together and fairly bear the burden of defending the Empire. Fewer wars, too, will occur in the world if the integrity of the British Empire be preserved.

" England unhappily lost her American Colonies just as they began to pass from infancy to maturity. Let us hope she will be more fortunate with those she at present possesses! God, in calling her to people the waste lands of the world, has conferred upon her a

[1] See Mr. Service and Sir Alex. Stuart's remarks, pages 181, 199.

great destiny—unparalleled among past nations, impossible among future nations.

"When we look at the past history and present condition of British colonization, we cannot but be amazed at the splendid vision, I should rather say splendid reality, that is before us. No portion of the history of England is more interesting or brilliant than that which records how this little island has, so to speak, been expanding herself over great continents, has been developing herself throughout the globe. Her language, her literature, her ideas, her commerce, her laws, her institutions, and her liberties, have been sown broadcast over the face of the earth; and already in different soils and in various climes they have borne magnificent fruits. But, splendid as the success of the past has been, splendid as the condition of the present is, the splendour, both of the past and of the present, seems destined to be dimmed by what we are justified in expecting in the future. We have, hitherto, only seen England nursing infant nations. I believe and ardently hope,—and I am certain I express the feelings of all her Colonies,—that she is destined to retain under her mild sway her Colonial children, long after they shall attain the maturity and the strength of manhood. I am convinced that the existence of such a relation will not only be of vast moral and material advantage, both to the parent nation and to the offspring nations, but will constitute an Empire more splendid than any the world has yet seen."

CHAPTER III.

PERMANENT UNITY OF THE EMPIRE.

Progress of the Imperial Question—Is it desirable that the Empire
shall remain permanently united ?—What must be the ultimate
bond of political union ?—How foreigners regard our Empire—
Fallacies of Disintegrationists and " Economists "—Professor
Goldwin Smith's views—Unionists true Economists—How
England and the Colonies would be affected by Separation—
Their position beside the United States—Naval strength of
the United Empire—Union means peace—Economic advantages—Protective and differential duties within Empire—
Foreign *octroi*—Danger to England from India and the
Colonies—Federation our ultimate goal—Separation of territories by oceans will facilitate Federation—Representation
of Colonies in present Imperial Parliament—A Colonial
Council—Ambassadors—Intercolonial more difficult than Imperial Federation—Irish Home Rule—Federal Parliament
and Executive indispensable—Non-interference with Provincial self-government—Federalists only have clear views as
to future—Imperial Federation the greatest of political questions—Momentous issues hang upon it—Should have definite
ideas about it—Burke's pictures of Colonial growth eclipsed—
Ripening of the policy.

In January, 1875, I endeavoured to set forth the reasons
for Unity and Federation, with a very brief outline
of the latter, before the Royal Colonial Institute, in
a paper entitled, "The Permanent Unity of the
Empire." With some slight alterations, it forms this
chapter, the argument thus proceeding :—

Those who watch with interest, the rapidly changing

conditions of the relations between England and her
Colonies, must be struck with the progress made
within five or six years, in what is popularly known
as the Colonial, but should more correctly be called
the Imperial, question. Within the period mentioned,
that question has been much more frequently discussed
than ever it was before, and has occupied a larger
share of the serious attention of intelligent men:
many doubts have been cleared up; what the question
really means is becoming more generally understood;
and the official tone of the Imperial Government
towards the Colonies has changed from ungenial
politeness to decided heartiness.

The Imperial question practically resolves itself into
two heads of inquiry: 1st. Is it desirable that the
Empire shall remain permanently united; and if so,
2nd, what must be the ultimate bond of political union
—the form of Government which is to weld it into
one great Power?

With regard to the first, nothing is more calculated
to excite the amazement of foreigners, who admire the
Empire of England and envy her its possession, than
that any Englishman should counsel, or even tacitly
countenance, any policy tending to its disintegration.

Is there a German who loves his country, from
Prince Bismarck down to the most insignificant
politician, who would not give much, and strive hard,
to make the new German Empire like our British
Empire, which some Englishmen think should be
allowed to fall to pieces? Though only a few
individuals may hold such an opinion, it is too true
of the nation, that "we do not sufficiently esteem
what we possess."

A few years ago, an attempt was made to form a

school, to teach, in the name of superior wisdom, that
our soundest policy is one which, within a generation
or two, would reduce the great British Empire to the
limits of these little islands. These teachers started
with Adam Smith's description of the unsound Colonial
policy of the past; and, seemingly, were so scared by
that old and unwise system as not to be content with
its abandonment; but they would have us run off so
far from it as to carry newer and wiser principles to
lengths equally unsound. Our grandfathers having
done unwise things, we are told to show how much
more sensible we are by rushing into the opposite
extreme; they having by a most fallacious policy
bound and shackled the Colonies, we should embrace
the opposite fallacy, and sever every tie connecting
them with England.

The Disunionist school has made but little way since
its master, Professor Goldwin Smith, propounded his
theses some dozen years ago.[1] Since he wrote, events
have belied his anticipations. His case is weaker
now than it even was when first stated. The expense
of the Colonies to this country has been greatly
reduced;[2] twelve years' growth has been added to
their strength, to their ability to defend themselves,
to the weight they could contribute to the power of
a consolidated Empire; wisely or unwisely, British
troops have been withdrawn from the Colonies;

[1] See letters in *Daily News*, 1862 and 1863, published in book
called "The Empire," 1863.
[2] Mr. Archibald Hamilton, in his paper read before the Statistical
Society, gives a table, which shows that the cost in 1870 and 1871,
the two lowest years, was £1,319,439 and £1,045,212 respectively,
and in 1864, the highest, £3,140,176. He also proves that in
nineteen years, from 1853 to 1871, the Imperial revenue derived
from the Colonial trade was £45,000,000, and the Imperial expenditure on the Colonies was only £43,000,000.

happily Canada has ceased to be a probable, and has become only a remotely possible, source of danger to this country. We have entered on an era of amity with the United States; and France, the only other nation that could possibly have assailed England in what we are told is her weakest point—her Colonies— has no longer the power even had she the will to do so.[1] The unworthy fears with which Professor Smith tried to frighten England, ingloriously to abandon her Colonial Empire, have become more unreal, and its continued growth and development must still more palpably prove them to have been baseless.

But if fear will not prevail with England, perhaps avarice may; so, in the name of economy, she is told to rid herself of her splendid heritage. The Empire does not "pay," and it is not worth having if its profits and advantages cannot be clearly demonstrated upon balance-sheets: no indirect claims of advantage can be admitted; nothing that cannot be computed in pounds, shillings, and pence. But to meet this so-called argument of economy upon its own low level. Even were the cost of the Colonies to England a few hundred thousand pounds a year, till they become able to bear the whole expense of their own defence, would not their independence at once increase the expenditure of this country in time of peace, there being no greater certainty of the cost and danger of war being lessened to England? Would she not have to pay ministers and consuls where she now sends governors at no cost whatever? Would she not have to maintain war-vessels to protect her commerce just as at present; but with the additional expense of having to form and keep up fortified harbours and coaling stations, instead

[1] In 1875 France was exhausted by the recent war.

of those like Sydney and Melbourne, now provided for
her by the Colonies, whose ports are as much hers in
time of peace, and would be as exclusively hers in war
—as hostile to her foes—as if situated in the United
Kingdom? Are not such advantages capable of
computation in a good round sum of money? Were
it necessary to do so, would it not even be wise in
England to spend for the next few years more than
she does upon Colonial defences, if afterwards the
Colonies, when more populous and powerful, would
contribute their due proportion to the joint defence
of the Empire? Those economists, who for the sake
of saving would get rid of the Colonial Empire, always
remind me of the illustrious Mr. Paterfamilias, whose
better half, and wiser half, is described as complaining
that her husband's savings were always so terribly
expensive.

The disintegrationist puts his case in another
equally unattractive aspect. He entirely agrees with
those who think it was wise of England to found
Colonies, and to keep them till they have passed a
certain stage of infancy; but when the time comes
that she can trade with them just as well if independent, he declares that the sooner they separate
from her the better. As to their being people of her
own blood and language, as to their union with her
adding to her prestige, it is all sentiment; we ought
to be superior to such moonshine. The only true
standard of value is money, the light to see everything in is the colour of gold, the glitter of sovereigns.
We have only to state this so-called economical argument in plain English to make it self-repellent.
England will never become such "a nation of shop-
keepers," in the worst sense of the term, as to be

utterly regardless of the great moral and material advantages she may derive, from preserving in union with herself, the whole of that Empire at the head of which Providence has placed her. Should the Decline and Fall of the British Empire have to be recorded by some future Gibbon, shall it be told to our perpetual shame that such a catastrophe was occasioned by a petty, peddling, penny-wise, pound-foolish policy?

But let us see if the advocates of the unity of the Empire have not the principles of true economy on their side. We have already seen that, for England the independence of the Colonies would permanently occasion expenses not at present existing, and would not insure her the certainty that wars would be of less danger and cost to her. The expenses of the Colonies, too, would be augmented by separation. They would have to organize a costly diplomatic and consular service, to largely increase their land and sea defences, to endeavour to create navies, unless they were content to trust for safety to their insignificance as tenth-rate powers. A certain permanent increase of expense, and no additional security, would therefore immediately accrue to them as well as to the Mother Country, were they to separate.

But what of the future? What will it be for England if she be isolated? The development of her manufactures within the present century, has given her a population she cannot feed, and for whose support she has to send abroad from £60,000,000 to £80,000,000 per annum. The cost of living has rapidly become more expensive, and must continue to increase; so that it is very doubtful if England will be able permanently to keep her population up to its present number. It is evident she cannot do so unless

her manufactures and trade continue as highly prosperous as they now are. Should they decline from
any cause, such, for instance, as the gradual exhaus-
tion of the supply of coal or iron, the inhabitants of
this country must considerably diminish. They can
never attain the number the United States will possess
within the lifetime of men now living. For England
to be separated from the rest of her Empire, will be
to remain stationary, or comparatively so, while new
countries grow up to and outstrip her in population,
wealth, and power. The United States have gained
considerably upon her within the last few years;
their inhabitants, according to the last census, numbering thirty-eight millions and a half.

Then, too, if the Colonies became independent, what
figure would they present beside this great young
power? When would Australia, great and populous
as she is destined to become, attain a position of anything like equality with America? She has not yet
two millions of inhabitants.[1] In what century, then,
could we expect the territories of the great Transatlantic
Republic to become so over-crowded, that the rate of
increase of population will be sufficiently checked to
allow Australia to overtake America?[2]

United in a great British Imperial Union, we shall
in the future stand in a position of equality beside the
American Union, or any other great power: divided,
neither England nor any of the Colonies, for generations, will be able to do so, and we must, at no
distant date, resign the leadership of the Anglo-Saxon
race to our American cousins. Far be it from us to
think the growth of the United States a danger to us,
or to regard them with the least jealousy. A laudable

[1] In 1875.   [2] See page 241.

pride, however, would make us desire and strive that in the future ours shall be a great British Empire, which, if its union be cemented, and power consolidated by means of some federal organization, may be as strong and influential—a British union which shall never be the foe, but always the friendly rival of the American Union, in carrying forward that civilization of the world which Providence seems to have destined the Anglo-Saxon race to accomplish. A French writer[1] has said that the world of the future will be Anglo-Saxon. If so, it will be better that the race shall form two great nations, than one first-class Power and a number of inferior States.[2]

It must obviously be much more economical in the future for England and the Colonies to contribute fair proportions to the defences of a United Empire, than for each separately to maintain its own. The ships—though for years of little account as the navies of independent States—which the different groups of Colonies could contribute to that maritime force which would be the chief strength of the Empire, would, acting together and with the fleets of England, make up a mighty and irresistible navy, with which we should be able to keep the oceans of the world free for our commerce, and to prescribe peace upon them.[3]

Another important economic consideration, to put it on the lowest ground, is that union will mean peace as well as strength ; for the greater the number of

---

[1] See pages 118, 151.

[2] To show that British Federalists entertain the reverse of hostility to the United States, I may mention that from first to last, during the Civil War, my sympathies were with the North, because I felt that any further division was most undesirable for the Anglo-Saxon race; and now I am more than ever convinced of the correctness of the opinion. See also pages 43, 145, 185, 213.

[3] See pages 71, 98, 140, 184, 213.

independent states in the world, particularly if they
be small ones, the more are the chances of war increased.
So great a power as the federated Empire would
become, would not be aggressive ; it would be large
enough not to covet its neighbours' dominions, and
strong enough not to feel that weakness which sometimes makes nations go to war to test their strength,
or to show they are not afraid to fight.[1]

We are sometimes told that the persistence of some
of the Colonies in the policy of protection will be fatal
to our permanent union, and some indignation was
expressed at the idea of the Australian Colonies wanting to adopt differential duties in each other's favour.
It would be easy to conceive of a Federation, even had
we no existing example of one in Switzerland, in
which the provincial governments might confer exclusive privileges upon local populations. Most objectionable as such a policy undoubtedly is, there is no
reason to prevent the States in which it obtains from
being united in a Federation. Continuance in union
is more likely to lead to the removal of such invidious
distinctions than separation, which must make them
permanent and more numerous. Would it not also
be better to recognize differences as to the truths
of free-trade than quarrel about them ? And—if we
can agree to continue united, and, for the purposes of
mutual support, weld ourselves into an Empire in
reality as well as in name—let us not think of disputing
the right of the provincial legislatures to adjust their
own revenues and manage their local affairs in their
own way ; and never seek to impose upon them, save
by the force of conviction, a uniform fiscal policy.
Were England to separate from the Colonies on account

[1] See page 184.

of protection, would they be as likely to adopt a different system as if she remain in union with them?

Adam Smith describes trade restrictions existing in his time, not only between these three kingdoms, but even between the people of England themselves, which were much more incompatible with the union of the same people under one central government, than any restrictions imposed by Colonial tariffs. To say that people of the same State cannot remain united and impose taxes upon each other, is also opposed to present experience. On the Continent, *octroi* duties are levied by towns, and free cities exist with exemptions from taxation not enjoyed by the rest of the State. But, however opposed to sound principles of political economy it may be, thus to favour particular communities in the same State, there is nothing in doing so inconsistent with their being united under one government. Now, in principle, the taxation of imports from other parts of the Empire, by the government of any of its provinces, is similar to the foreign *octroi*, and the favour shown by some Colonies to their own productions is sufficiently analogous, for my argument, to the system of free cities or ports. Therefore, however strongly we may disapprove of protection, we should be unreasonable in our condemnation of it were we to hold that it must make all the difference, between our permanent union being possible or impossible, desirable or undesirable.

The wish of contiguous Colonies to adopt differential duties in each other's favour is perfectly reasonable, and only the existence of protection could excite anything like hostility to the idea. It is extremely inconvenient for Colonies, like those of Australia, with artificial boundary lines hundreds of miles long, often in unpeopled regions, to keep up a strict custom-house system; and, without desiring to make any distinction to the disadvantage of their fellow-subjects in other parts of the Empire, they may well seek to modify or abolish it, levying duties—whether free trade or protectionists—only upon imports from the seaboard. It is quite a different matter, and would be incompatible with the Imperial relation, to allow differential duties and reciprocity treaties, between provinces of the Empire and governments outside it, whereby foreign goods should be admitted on terms more favourable than those extended to British trade.

Every available argument by which it is attempted to prove continued union with the Colonies undesirable for England, and many weighty reasons besides, may be applied with greater force to the possession of India. Indeed, Professor Goldwin Smith has declared the acquisition of that country to have been a mistake, and that its abandonment would be desirable, could England with honour free herself from the obligations she has contracted to govern it. And, certainly, India has been in the past, and is likely to prove in the future, a more fruitful source of danger and disaster to England than the Colonies ever were, or can possibly become.

Were the people of England and of the Colonies to be persuaded—by those who counsel them, with arguments of fear or of avarice—to abandon the Empire, Burke's famous hyperbolical sentence would become literally true of them—"the age of chivalry is gone. That of sophisters, economists, and calculators has succeeded; and the glory of Europe is extinguished for ever."

Having, as far as the space I can afford to that head of my subject will permit, touched upon the leading points showing that the permanent union of the Empire is desirable, and having endeavoured to prove the objections to it to be unworthy and unreal, I shall now, as briefly as possible, consider what form of Imperial government will ultimately be indispensable. The more permanent bonds of union which will be required, when the Colonies attain a more mature growth, are still too little thought of by most reformers of Imperial relations; who continue considering what will be wanted for the short transition period, between the infancy and maturity of the Colonies, forgetting that that period is rapidly passing away, while they leisurely devise policies for it which, if ever matured, will never be needed.

That cannot be called statesmanship which would only deal with the Colonial question of the moment. It is time to think what may be required twenty, thirty, fifty years hence, and shape our policy accordingly. We may wisely determine what direction to take, and steadily steer in it, even if the point for which we are bound be many a long day distant from us. The only ultimate goal for us, if the union of our Empire is to be real and lasting, is Federation. "Political inventiveness" may possibly produce new systems of government, but that is the only known form which can weld the Empire into one great power—giving all its people a voice in whatever policy concerns them, and utilizing for their peace and security the great strength which, if solidified, they will be able to command.

Federation implies that there shall be a central Parliament and Executive of the Empire, like those of

America, Germany, or Switzerland. I have endeavoured to sketch out a system of Federation, the outlines of which are, I believe, capable of being filled in. The subject is dealt with in the next chapter.

The only obstacle suggested to our federal union not affecting existing Federations, is that oceans would roll between its several portions, and that its extremities would be more remote than those of other Federations. In reply it may be asked, Is the federal union of Canada with England impossible, because Canadian representatives would have to cross the Atlantic in steamers, whilst that of California with the United States is quite practicable, because representatives have to make about an equally long journey by railway from San Francisco to Washington? And would the fact that the voyage from Australia to England takes six weeks or two months, instead of a week or fortnight, make all the difference between Federation being practicable and impracticable?

In fact, the separation of its territories by sea might even strengthen a federal union, by necessitating less interference with provincial self-government. For instance, the Western and Eastern States of America seriously differ about free-trade and protection; and both being on the same mainland, each cannot have the policy it prefers. If a sea were to separate them, they might have different tariffs, and thus a danger to the Federation would be removed without its strength as a great power being impaired.

In a paper on the Colonies in the "Cobden Club Essays," Professor Thorold Rogers takes the same view of the objection of distance as that for which I have now contended, and also in my paper on "Imperial and Colonial Federalism." Speaking of Colonial re-

presentation in the British Parliament, he says: " There
is no difficulty in carrying out the project, because the
Colony is distant from the seat of government;" and
that Federation "would be undertaken if the British
Parliament were less of a Chamber in which peddling
interests were discussed and settled by compromise,
and more of a Senate where great questions of policy
were debated and determined." Professor Rogers, like
many others, rejects the idea of Federation because he
conceives it to mean representation of the Colonies in
the present British Parliament. And certainly they
could expect but little benefit, from having a few
members in an Assembly, which almost exclusively
devotes itself to the provincial concerns of the United
Kingdom, and in which really Imperial questions are
liable to be decided by a count-out. To give all parts
of the Empire a voice in its government, an exclusively
Imperial Parliament would be required. The present
Parliament occupies itself with the concerns of Great
Britain and Ireland, which monopolize its attention
and supply it with more business than it can conveniently get through. Representation of the Colonies
in it could not be made sufficiently federal in its
character, unless the number of members of the House
of Commons, already large enough, were increased, or
those for the United Kingdom diminished, in order to
make room for a due proportion of Colonial representatives. Neither would it be desirable that in those
numerous questions exclusively affecting these kingdoms, any but their own representatives should take
part. The only conceivable advantage of having a
few members for the Colonies in the British Parliament
would be, that their presence would be an admission
of the federal principle, and might demonstrate the

necessity, and stimulate the desire throughout the Empire for a complete Federation.

An Imperial Council like that for India is another expedient, suggested by some who do not yet see their way to Federation. But, of whatever value such an institution might for the present be, it would be perfectly inadequate as a permanent central governing body for the Empire. It could be entrusted with no powers of legislation or of raising an Imperial revenue; it would give the Colonies no such real voice in Imperial policy as that to which their increasing populations will render them entitled. In fact, the proposals to have Colonial representatives in Parliament, an Imperial Council, Colonial members of the Privy Council, and Secretaries of State sent by the Colonies to sit in the English cabinet, must all, however valuable they might be for a time, prove only temporary expedients, not to be recommended, but as means to produce something much more complete and permanent. Their existence would soon demonstrate their own insufficiency; and the only good to be hoped from them would be that they might assist to create, and then make way for, a real federal organization.[1]

From the list of possible suggestions just referred to, I think the proposal should be excluded that the Colonies should have in this country representatives, similar to the ambassadors sent by Foreign Powers. As one born and brought up in the Colonies, I should strongly object to anything sounding and looking so like Colonial independence. May the most marked

[1] The idea of having a Council was some time ago revived by Earl Grey and met with considerable favour; but Sir Hercules Robinson and Lord Augustus Loftus have ably set forth the view I had previously endeavoured to express, that a Council will be quite inadequate as a federal bond of union.

distinction ever exist between foreign ministers and
the representatives of the Colonies in this country,
whatever may be their status !

It may perhaps be said, How can we expect Colonies
to agree to the greater scheme of Federation, with the
Mother-Country and the rest of the Empire, when their
jealousies prevent them from forming federal unions
among themselves? Canada would not have united
herself in a Federation had she not felt the need of
that strength which union alone could give her;
Australia, not so urgently feeling the want of a federal
government, has not been as anxious to form one,
though it would be of undoubted advantage to her.
The objection seems capable of being more briefly
answered than stated. Federation implies a certain
amount of concession, and young communities may
resolutely refuse to give way to each other, though
they would not have the slightest hesitation in yield-
ing precedence to the old country; so that really it
would probably be more easy to form an Imperial than
an inter-Colonial Federation. Besides, the Colonies
would feel that it would add to their prestige to be
taken into council, to be admitted to a share with the
old country in the government of the Empire.

Imperial Federalism and Irish Home Rule are in no
way necessarily connected. The latter is a question
with which the inhabitants of the United Kingdom
should alone be left to deal.[1]

The whole sum of the matter seems to be, that the
maintenance of the unity of the Empire is desirable,
and consequently a central government will be required to represent all its portions, giving each that
weight which, from its importance and the share it

[1] See pages 21, 69, 108, 196.

will take in the defence of the Empire, shall be its
due in all Imperial questions, such as peace, war,
defence, foreign affairs. If this is to be effected, our
children, if not ourselves, must see the establishment
of a real Federation with a Parliament and Executive,
as distinct from and superior to those of England and
of the different Colonies, as the new Legislature and
Government of United Germany, are distinct from
and superior to the Chambers and Ministries of Prussia
and Bavaria, or the federal governments of the American Union or of Switzerland are distinct from and
superior to those of the States or Cantons of which
these Federations are respectively composed. Such a
federal government need not interfere with the present
full and free control of the provincial governments
over local affairs. We should not perhaps at first
attempt to set up a very complete federal government.
Our object may probably be best reached, by beginning
with the simplest form of Federation we can devise—
perhaps one of those systems which I have spoken of
as temporary expedients—always keeping in view and
moving forward towards something more perfect; for
the history of federalism in America, Germany, and
Switzerland, where it has had greater and more serious
difficulties to surmount than any it will with us have
to encounter, shows that the tendency of the system
when once it is planted, is to take root, grow, and
ripen into greater perfection. Its introduction among
us would, assuredly, create throughout our Empire an
enthusiasm for and loyalty to our union, as strong as
that of Americans for theirs, when it became apparent
to what a position Federation would elevate both
England and the Colonies,—what strength, what greatness, what security, what peace it would, with the

blessing of God, ensure us. Proud as we all are of the glorious old Union Jack, of being British subjects, how much more proud might we justly be, could we regard that flag as the emblem of a still greater union, could we call ourselves citizens of a still greater British Empire, of an Imperial Federation of which the Sovereign of England should be head.

I have endeavoured to give a slight sketch of a question upon which many volumes may be written. Federation is, I believe, a perfectly practicable policy for the future, if we only maintain and develop, throughout the Empire, the strong Imperial spirit and warm affection for the great principle of unity, of which we find in various quarters so many happy indications. Without Federation I cannot conceive how we can ultimately get on; how we can give our new and rising communities the voice in Imperial affairs, to which a few years' additional growth will entitle them; how we can combine our defences and utilize our strength as one great united Power. The Federalists alone show how all this can be effected; they, and they only, have a clear, definite, and satisfactory policy for the future. Those who reject that policy suggest positively nothing instead. They can see their way for no distance before them, and can only hope that, out of the mist in which they are involved, they may, somehow or other, stumble upon a right track.

In the region of politics, this question towers immeasurably above all others in importance and grandeur; it is the greatest which statesmanship can ever touch. Upon its skilful handling depends nothing less than the momentous issue whether, within a century, the greatest Empire the world can ever see shall be made or marred. The thought is supremely impressive. In its presence, all petty provincialisms, strifes, jealousies, party differences, should shrink into fitting insignificance. England by an unhappy policy lost her first Colonies; she has now a second great opportunity—such as never before fell to the lot of a nation, and certainly can never occur again—of permanently fixing her borders far beyond her narrow sea-girt isles, and incorporating in indissoluble union with these ancient kingdoms, vast new dominions in various climes and in different hemispheres.

Seeing, then, that the question of its permanent unity is of such vital importance to our whole British race, it is time to think of and form some definite ideas and plans for its future organization. Nothing could be more practical. Only on the most superficial, shallow view of the question, can it be said not to be so, or that we ought to postpone beginning to think of it. Postpone, indeed, considering this question! with Canada progressing as she is, with Australia almost doubling her population in a dozen years, with South Africa advancing with increasing speed, with the whole Empire growing so rapidly, that only in the eloquent language of the famous Burke can we find words to describe its progress: "Fiction lags after truth; invention is unfruitful, and imagination cold and barren;" and in another passage: "For my part, I never cast an eye on their flourishing commerce, and their cultivated and commodious life, but they seem to me to be rather ancient nations grown to perfection through a long series of fortunate events, and a train of successful industry, accumulating wealth in many centuries, than the Colonies of yesterday."

That great statesman, and perhaps greatest of

orators—whose words are even more descriptive of our present circumstances than they were of those to which he applied them—may be said to have been the father of the great principle of Imperial unity, which his immortal speeches unmistakably breathe forth. Those who reflect so little on the progress of the past, and have so far failed to learn from it the lessons it should teach respecting the future—as to tell us it is too soon to speak and think about Imperial organizations—should study Burke's grand picture of the progress of the British Empire of his time, in which he describes how the commerce of England to her Colonies alone had grown in 1772 to £6,509,000, only £485,000 less than the whole export trade of England in 1704.

With as much truth as eloquence Burke spoke of this sixty-eight years of the progress of England and her Colonies. How, were he now living, would he describe the much greater progress of a much shorter period? How would he speak of the sure development of the next few years? What a theme the permanent unity of our present Empire would be for him! How his eloquent voice would be raised against the ignoble idea of disintegration! How it would arouse those who sleep over, and leave unthought of, the great question of the future organization of our union!

I must, in conclusion, expressly guard myself against the charge of wishing to see Federation forced on before its time,—and upon this point I believe all Imperial Federalists are agreed. Nothing is further from our desire; few things could be more fatal to our object. We do not think of plucking the fruit before it is ripe; but we do want this question, and the public opinion of the Empire respecting it, to grow and ripen in due season, under the healthy and maturing influences of timely consideration and discussion.

We may well commend a cause, so noble and so pure, to " Him who raises and pulls down nations at His pleasure," and pray that " the Author of peace and Lover of concord " may bless and preserve the unity of our Empire.

CHAPTER IV.

MODES OF FEDERATION SUGGESTED.

Order of argument—Influence of national magnetism—Shall we
furnish exception to unity of kindred people?—Unity of
Germany and Italy—Forethought required—The more good
plans suggested the better—Many plans of Federation—Suggestions at Conference of 1871—Two modes of electing
Imperial Parliament: directly by people of Empire, *i.e.* Federation, or by Provincial Parliaments, *i.e.* Confederation—One
or two Chambers?—How an Upper House might be constituted
—A grand Imperial Senate—British Federation with least
amount of change in present Imperial Parliament—Most
elementary Federal systems—Were Senate only Federal body
in America and Bundesrath in Germany?

IN order of date, the ideas contained in the first part
of this chapter should come before those of my paper
on "The Permanent Unity of the Empire," reproduced in the last, but in order of argument they
come in their proper place—the reasons for unity and
federation preceding any plan for carrying out the
latter. Between producing "The Future Relations
of England and her Colonies" in 1869, and "The
Permanent Unity of the Empire" in 1875, I had
become a firm believer in the policy of Imperial
Federation—in 1871 sketching out the following plan,[1]
as one of many which might be suggested. Leading up
to it were observations of which these formed part:—

[1] In a paper entitled, "Imperial and Colonial Federalism," read
at the Westminster Conference on Colonial Questions, July 20,
1871, and published in "Discussions on Colonial Questions."

At first sight, a federal union of the British Empire may, perhaps, be regarded as a grand but impracticable idea. But, though public attention has only recently been called to it, many people have already been brought to believe in it. It has made so much progress in so short a time that its friends have much to hope from its further discussion. The tendencies of the times favour it. National magnetism has wrought wonders in our days, in drawing together people of the same blood and language; it is one of the most powerful influences of the age. Dynastic interests and provincial jealousies which have stood stubbornly for ages, walling off countrymen from countrymen, have yielded to it in Germany and Italy. Shall we, then, be told that it will be more difficult for us, who are united, to remain so, and to cement our union, than for those who have been separated for generations to become united? While the ties of all the other great families of the human race are becoming stronger, shall those of ours grow weaker and fall asunder? Shall we furnish the only exception to the rule of the unity of kindred people?

To bring about non-existing union, Germany required one of the greatest statesmen and one of the highest military geniuses the world has produced. Italy also needed a statesman of like calibre; and both countries only succeeded by means of Titanic wars. We shall not want a Moltke; and were the peaceful process, of cementing and organizing our existing union, a task only possible for the greatest of statesmen to accomplish, we might well expect that some of the old or new lands of the Empire would produce for us a Bismarck or a Cavour.

Procrastinators forget the rate at which events have

been hastening. They do not bear in mind how far we have got from the recent past. It seems an age, though it was only yesterday, since the question of Colonial self-government had not advanced beyond the stage of discussion.[1] Twenty years ago it was a matter for consideration whether the Colonies were mature enough to take care of their own affairs. Before another twenty years have passed away, subjects of still greater importance must be settled; for Colonial growth is so rapid that the mere speculations of to-day will be practical questions urgently requiring solution to-morrow; and a wise forethought would suggest that we should think leisurely upon these things; so that when their settlement can be put off no longer, we shall not have to arrive at hurried conclusions.

The question of the future relations of England and her Colonies, has grown so fast during the last few months, that it is fairly pushing its way into the front rank of important questions. Even in very recent discussions of Colonial affairs, the word "Federation" does not appear, ideas not having advanced beyond the suggestion of reform in the Colonial Office, and the creation of a Colonial Council like that for India.

In dealing with this important subject, it seems expedient that we should not so much desire to win approval for any particular plan, as to have as many plans as possible passed in review; so that it may be evident that there are more ways than one in which our great purpose of cementing the union of the Empire may be attained. This Conference, I remarked, had only one policy—the unity of the Empire. Every plan, every suggestion, made with a view to that end

---

[1] This was in 1871.

is acceptable. Every other consideration should be made subservient to it. We are not here to advocate any particular mode of carrying out this great policy, but simply to suggest. In this spirit it is the design of my paper to treat this question. Though I may have a favourite plan of federation, I should be sorry to think it the only one possible. The larger the number of good systems, that can be suggested, the better we should be pleased. If we thoroughly believe in our great principle, discussion of details alone is needed to ensure a successful organization.

Two systems of Federation may be suggested, both providing a Parliament, in which the whole Empire could be represented; the one under which the members representing the United Kingdom and the Colonies in the Parliament of the Empire, would be elected directly by the people—that would be Federation; and the other, under which they would be chosen by the English Parliament and the Colonial Parliaments, acting as electoral Colleges—that would be Confederation.[1] Were the latter system adopted, each Provincial Parliament could choose a certain number of members, or where Colonies were grouped in Federations, as in Canada, the Parliament of the Colonial Federation would elect the members; and, thus, were Australia and South Africa to follow the example of Canada, and were the West Indies also formed into an Intercolonial Federation, the government of the Empire would be a Confederation of

---

[1] Federation may be defined as a National or Imperial government, in which there is direct representation of the peoples of the Provinces or of the Interprovincial federations; Confederation, as a government in which only their governments are represented. See also page 94, for Professor Freeman's definition of Federation, and what Mr. Willoughby says, quoted at page 84.

Federations, with five constituencies electing the Imperial Parliament—namely, the English Parliament and the federal Parliaments of Australia, Canada, South Africa, and the West Indies.[1]

The system of election by Parliaments would, perhaps, be more easily worked, and there might be less difficulty in allotting the number of members, to be chosen by each Province or Colony of the Empire. A greater number of first-class men would be more likely to be returned to the Imperial Parliament; for each Provincial legislature would pride itself on sending some of its most distinguished members to the Parliament of the Empire. Again, the representatives of each province or dominion would be in harmony with its Legislature, which might not always be so were they returned by direct popular election.

This latter system, however, would have the more than countervailing advantage, of bringing the Imperial Federal Parliament into direct touch with the inhabitants of the whole Empire, making them feel that its central government was thoroughly their own. Peace or war, made with the approval of that government, would be their peace or war; defences organized by it would be felt to belong to them all. It would be able directly to impose Imperial taxes; whereas, if elected by the Legislatures, it could do no more than fix the amount of the subsidies by which they should make up the revenue of the Empire.

It would have to be considered whether the Imperial Parliament should consist of one or two Chambers. If the Provincial, or Intercolonial Federal, Parliaments were to elect the Imperial Parliament, and were an

---

[1] See Austro-Hungarian system, page 78.

F

Imperial Upper House deemed essential, it might be constituted by the Upper Houses of such Parliaments sending members to it, as the Lower Houses would do to the Imperial Lower House; or by the Crown being empowered to nominate a House, consisting of hereditary or life peers; or the members might be partly nominated and partly elected by the English and Colonial Parliaments. It is very satisfactory to think that in forming an Imperial Upper House, as well as in framing a Constitution for the Empire, we should not be limited to one plan. Were the people of the Empire directly the electors of the Imperial Parliament, it would be more necessary to have a second Chamber than if the Parliaments were the electors. With the Provincial Chambers thus acting as electoral Colleges, provision might be made for the representation, in the Imperial Parliament, of their minorities or oppositions.

If the principle of direct popular election were adopted, the questions of the franchise and electoral divisions, by which the members of the Imperial Lower House should be chosen, would be best left to be arranged in each Province or Intercolonial Federation by its Parliament, it being only necessary that the Imperial Federal Constitution should fix the number of members to be chosen by each Dominion or Province. The time for which the members of the Imperial Lower House should be elected ought perhaps not to exceed three years.

With a Parliament of the Empire, an Executive would be required; and in order that there might be statesmen to select from, it would be necessary that the Parliament should at least contain two hundred members.

Subsequently, in a letter published in 1876, in

Mr. (now Sir Frederick) Young's valuable book on "Imperial Federation," I ventured upon another suggestion as to the creation of an Imperial Senate or House of Lords—namely, that a certain proportion of its present hereditary peers could represent the United Kingdom in this great Imperial Senate, as life members—half might be chosen by the House of Lords. For pre-eminently distinguished services, however, the Crown might have power to confer the supreme distinction of a hereditary peerage of the Empire on any of its subjects. The Colonial members of the Senate could be created for life, by the Crown on the nomination of the Colonial Executives, and although only life legislators, might have titles derived from places in their Colonies. A certain number of Colonial statesmen from each Colony or Intercolonial Federation, who had made up a given number of years' service as responsible ministers, might be entitled to seats in the Imperial Upper House.

A Senate of the Empire, constituted as suggested, would be about the most brilliant legislative assembly that could be formed. It would consist of picked men from the hereditary peerage of England, and from the aristocracy of intellect and statesmanship of the whole British Empire. The hereditary peerage of the Empire would open up to that of the United Kingdom a still further avenue of distinction; and to be a life peer of this great Senate would be a great prize open to the statesmen of all our Colonies.

Should general opinion favour a Parliament of one Chamber, the Britannic Constitution could dispense with a second more easily than could that of any other federal union, for, as we shall see,[1] when we come

---

[1] At pages 95–114.

to the division of Imperial and Provincial questions, all property interests, such as those of capital and ownership of land, for which the protection of an Upper House is chiefly needed, would not be under the control of the Empire Parliament, but of those of the Dominions or Provinces. Mr. Howard Willoughby, in his "Australian Federation,"[1] affirms that "in a federal government a Senate is a necessity" to carry out "the principle that the States must be represented as well as the people."

An Imperial Parliament, whether of one or two Chambers, recruited from the wide field of talent, which our Empire would afford, ought to command the largest proportion of legislative and administrative ability it would be possible to collect, and would be fully capable of directing the vast world-wide, common concerns of the greatest of Empires.

It would of course be desirable that the Federation of the Empire should be effected, with as little change as possible in the constitution of the existing Imperial Parliament. I pointed out this in a letter published in the *Times*, August 18, 1886, in these terms—

"What, on the lines of existing federations and of our own Constitutional system, will be required if we are to have complete federation? Certainly an Imperial Parliament and Executive. We have at present a so-called Imperial Parliament, representing the thirty millions of these isles, but in which the ten millions of our British fellow-subjects beyond the seas have not a single member. The least sweeping Reform Bill, whereby these latter could be 'brought within the pale of the Constitution,' would be one which, without increasing the members of the House of Commons, would redistribute the seats in it, so as to give a proper proportion of them to the Colonies,

[1] Published in Melbourne, 1891.

and would place Colonial life peers in the House of Lords. The provincial concerns of the United Kingdom, which so clog and overwork the present composite Imperial-Provincial Parliament, and impede its action in all the general affairs of the Empire, would of course have to be entirely handed over to a Provincial Parliament and Executive. . . . The above is the briefest sketch, without details, how, on the most practical constitutional lines, with the least amount of changes, it would be possible to establish Imperial Federation."

Thus, Mr. John Morley's fear that " the Mother of Parliaments would sink to the condition of a State legislature," need not be realized. The old Imperial Parliament would continue to be the legislature of the Empire, confining itself exclusively to Imperial affairs, and handing over those of these kingdoms to a new one to be created for the purpose. There would be less change involved in this than there was in the creation of the present German and Austro-Hungarian federations or in the parliamentary union between England and Scotland, or Ireland and Great Britain, or in the establishment of constitutional government in the Colonies, or of Federation in Canada. None of these were revolutionary measures, but the adaptation of existing institutions to expanded national requirements. Supporters and opponents of Home Rule for Ireland, will agree that it would effect more serious and extensive changes in the British Isles, than would be involved in their federation, for common purposes, with the dominions of the Empire beyond the seas.

From the distinct forms of Federation suggested in this chapter, and the actual working systems described in the next, Federalism may be gradually shaded off to vanishing-point. This is reached by those who only want a mere Council of Advice, like that for India, which no more federates that country with Great

Britain, than would a similar council for the Colonies, federate them with the Mother Country. All that such a body could do is, no doubt, now practically done by the Agents-General. Federalism, though very elastic, cannot be stretched further than to include within its pale, such a very elementary representative body as the Colonial Conference which met in London in 1887. Nearer to full Federation would come such a system of Confederation as would exist, if the American Congress only consisted of the Senate, and the German Parliament of the Bundesrath, representing the State Governments of the respective unions, without there being any Chamber chosen by the people. It would, no doubt, be possible for the United States and Germany, to have their foreign affairs and defences managed by such a system of Confederation, instead of by the Federations they now have; but would it work as well, and would such a form of union be preferable for our Empire,—ultimately, even if it were so to begin with? In America, the Senate supervises foreign affairs, its sanction being required to ratify treaties, and war cannot be declared without the consent of Congress; neither can it be by the German Emperor without that of the Bundesrath. Such functions could of course be performed by these two federal bodies, or by any similar one which might be consti-tuted for our Empire, without the existence of a Chamber directly representing the people; but powers of raising revenue, even much more limited than those conferred by the German Constitution, could not be entrusted to the Central Government. Had we such a Confederate Council—for it would not be a Federal Parliament—it would only be able to administer, as an Executive, the revenue placed at its disposal, through the subsidies voted by the Parliaments of the Governments represented in such Confederate Council; which would fail in the purpose of its existence, unless always kept supplied with ample means, to maintain the foreign relations, common concerns, and defensive forces—above all the powerful navy, which would be essential to the security, strength, and very life of the Empire. Were we to start with such a Confederation, it would probably soon be found that it must be converted into a Federation of the American or German type.

There is clearly no need to formulate any more theoretical, detailed plans of union for our Empire, with such examples of Federation at work in the world. British Federalism is no mere theory, no original idea. Its advocates are mere copyists, not speculative, but practical men, desiring the adoption, or *adaption*, by our Empire of a well-proved system of government. When told that "no practical plan of Imperial Federation has ever been proposed," they have a conclusive answer, by merely referring to the systems brought side by side, for comparison, in the next chapter. We want no new "theories of government," for, as Thomas Carlyle says, "such have been and will be, in ages of decadence."

CHAPTER V.

FIVE EXISTING FEDERATIONS.

Canon Dalton on the existing Federal constitutions—The Federated Dominion of Canada—Federal and non-Federal questions separated—Chief points in the Constitution—Federation
of the United States—Makes great power of provinces of small
individual importance—Principal heads of Union—Federal
Union of Germany required to preserve ancient dynasties and
divisions—The Federal Parliament, revenue, etc.—The Austro-
Hungarian Union shows value of Federation in combining
distinct races for common defence—The most complicated
form of Federation—Austria a Federation federated with
Hungary—Leading provisions of the governments—Switzerland, smallest and oldest Federation—Too much machinery
of government—Instance of New Zealand—Particulars of
Swiss Federal Constitution—Federal Constitution framed by
Australian Convention—Leading features of it—Questions
to be taken over from provincial governments—Federalism,
monarchical and republican—Great success of system.

WERE a Conference convoked, representing the constitutional governments of the Empire—with whom
alone the framing of any federal organization must
rest—it would need to have no cut-and-dried schemes
prepared beforehand; for the practical statesmen, of
whom it would be composed, would find sufficient
models from which to work, in the provisions of the
federal constitutions now to be considered.

In 1884, the Rev. Canon Dalton, by an article in
the *Nineteenth Century*, did good service to the cause
of British Federalism, in placing side by side the

provisions of the different existing Federal constitutions. Those of Canada, the United States, Germany, Austria, Hungary, and Switzerland are models from which—if an exact copy, as a constitution for the Empire of Great Britain, could not be made—various modifications might be adopted to meet our Imperial requirements.

Canada, our own great British federated dominion, is an example of how federal can be separated from non-federal questions,[1] how the respective revenues of

[1] The act of Union thus divides the subjects to be dealt with by the Federal and Provincial Governments respectively. It will be observed that, with oceans separating our territories, many of the questions here placed in the first list might, in an Imperial Federal Constitution, be transferred to the second, as will be seen in next chapter.

Canadian Federal Questions.—1. Public debt and property. 2. Regulation of trade and commerce. 3. Raising of money by any mode or system of taxation. 4. Borrowing of money on public credit. 5. Postal services. 6. Census and statistics. 7. Military and naval service, militia, and defence. 8. Providing salaries of civil and other officers of the government of Canada. 9. Beacons, buoys, lighthouses, and Sable Island. 10. Navigation and shipping. 11. Quarantine and marine hospitals. 12. Sea coast and inland fisheries. 13. Ferries between a province and any British or foreign country. 14. Currency and coinage. 15. Banks, and the issue of paper money. 16. Savings' banks. 17. Weights and measures. 18. Bills of exchange and promissory notes. 19. Interest. 20. Legal tender. 21. Bankruptcy and insolvency. 22. Patents of invention. 23. Copyrights. 24. Indians and Indian reserves. 25. Naturalization and aliens. 26. Marriage and divorce. 27. Procedure in criminal law. 28. Penitentiaries.

Questions under control of Canadian Provincial Governments.— 1. Amendment of the constitution of the province, except as regards office of Lieut.-Governor. 2. Direct taxation within the province for revenue for provincial expenses. 3. Borrowing money on the sole credit of the provinces. 4. Establishment and tenure of provincial offices and the appointment and payment of provincial officers. 5. Management and sale of the public lands belonging to the province, and of the timber and wood thereon. 6. Establishment, maintenance, and management of hospitals, asylums, charities, and eleemosynary institutions in and for the province other than marine hospitals. 7. Establishment, maintenance, and management of public and reformatory prisons in and for the province. 8. Municipal institutions in the provinces. 9.

dominion and provinces can be raised, and how representation in the government of the former can be
satisfactorily given to the latter. "The British North
American" Act of the Imperial Parliament, passed in
1867,[1] created a Federal Parliament and responsible
ministry. The Upper House or Senate consists of 80
members, who are nominated for life by the Governor-
General; 24 each for Ontario and Quebec; 10 each
for Nova Scotia and New Brunswick; 4 for Prince
Edward's Island; 3 each for Manitoba and British
Columbia; and 2 for the North-west Territories. The
Dominion House of Commons, of 213 members, will
give, according to the census of 1891, one to every
22,688 inhabitants; or, to Ontario, 92; Quebec, 65;
Nova Scotia, 20; New Brunswick, 14; British Columbia,

Shop, saloon, tavern, auctioneer, and other licences, in order to
the raising of revenue for provincial, local, or municipal purposes.
10. Local works and undertakings other than such as are of the
following classes:—(*a*) Lines of steam or other ships, railways,
canals, telegraphs, and other works and undertakings, connecting
the provinces with any other or others of the provinces, or extending beyond the limits of the provinces; (*b*) Lines of steamships
between the provinces and any British or foreign country; (*c*) Such
works as, although wholly situate within the province, are before
or after their execution declared by the Parliament of Canada to
be for the general advantage of Canada, or for the advantage of
two or more of the provinces. 11. Incorporation of companies with
provincial objects. 12. Solemnization of marriage in the province.
13. Property and civil rights in the province. 14. Administration
of justice in the provinces, including the constitution, maintenance,
and organization of provincial courts both of civil and criminal
jurisdiction, and including proceedings in civil matters in those
courts. 15. Imposition of punishment by fine, penalty, or im-
prisonment for enforcing any law of the province made in relation
to any matter coming within any of the classes of subjects enumerated in this section. The provincial legislatures exclusively make
laws as to education, subject to specified limitations.

[1] The steps leading to the introduction of the Bill are briefly
noticed at page 225. For full particulars of the Act, and everything relating to it, see "Constitution of Canada," by Mr. Joseph
Doutre, Q.C., of the Montreal bar. Rev. W. P. Greswell's
"History of the Dominion of Canada" gives a shorter account.

6; Prince Edward's Island, 5; Manitoba, 6; and North-west Territories, 4. The possession of one of several small electoral qualifications confers the franchise.

The Provincial governments are not alike; Quebec, Nova Scotia, New Brunswick, and Prince Edward's Island having two Houses of Legislature, but Ontario, British Columbia, and Manitoba only one. All have Governors—appointed for five years by the Governor-General—and responsible ministers.

The Federal Dominion was originally formed of only four provinces: Ontario, Quebec, Nova Scotia, and New Brunswick. The others joined afterwards, Newfoundland still remains outside the union. The whole Empire would, probably, not come into Imperial Federal Union at first.

The neighbouring Anglo-Saxon federation of the United States [1] is the most remarkable instance, showing how a number of self-governing provinces—none of which by itself would form an independent State of any consideration in the world—may, by federal union for common purposes, make themselves into one of the greatest of Powers. The election of the President need not be noticed, as happily having no bearing upon our subject; for our union would not be troubled by periodical contests for the office of its chief. The President's ministers are not responsible to the House of Representatives, but to him. The Senate, consisting

---

[1] Those who want the history, instead of a mere outline, of American federation, can study it as it was—when it just came fresh, as a theory, from the minds of its originators—in the pages of "The Federalist," written in 1788 by Alexander Hamilton, Madison and Jay, and as it is now—after a century's practical working—described in Professor Bryce's great work, "The American Commonwealth," published in 1888.

of two members from every State, is chosen at a joint meeting of both Houses, by each legislature of the forty-two States which now compose the Union. The number of members which each State is entitled to return to the House of Representatives, is adjusted by the census taken every ten years. In 1880, with a population of 50,000,000, and a House of 332 members, the proportion was one to every 152,000 inhabitants; in 1890, with 62,000,000, and 356 members, it was fixed at one to every 174,000.

The questions which are Federal and which are Provincial are clearly defined by the Constitution. The governments of the numerous States are very much alike; each has a Governor, elected for two or three years, and two Houses of Legislature, called by different names in different States, the number of members in the Upper Houses being small. The Governor has control of the militia.

The Federal Congress levies and collects taxes and duties, which are uniform in the States, regulates defence, commercial relations, coinage, weights, measures, post-office, patents, etc., and has power to make peace and war. Congress, by majorities of two-thirds of both Houses, may propose alterations of the Constitution, or, on application from two-thirds of the State Legislatures, shall call a convention for the purpose. Amendments, proposed in either way, become law, when confirmed by three-fourths of the States, or by Conventions in three-fourths of them—whichever mode of ratification Congress may decide shall be adopted.

Turning to Europe, Germany has a Federal Government, not because the area of her territory renders it indispensable,—for a single Executive and Parliament might, as in France, conduct her internal and external affairs—but because Federation was required to preserve what she does not wish to abolish, namely, the ancient dynasties and divisions of the country; which could not have been got rid of without a revolution so sweeping that, rather than have recourse to it, the sober-minded Germans would, probably, have foregone the advantages of national unity.

The Federal Parliament is composed of an Upper and Lower House. The former, called the Bundesrath, or Federal Council, numbers 58 members, who represent the governments of the several States, by which they are appointed for each session. The Reichstag, of 397 members, represents the people of Germany, being elected for five years by universal suffrage. There is one member for every 124,500 inhabitants. The following is the representation of the larger States—

	In the Bundesrath.	In the Reichstag.
Prussia	17	236
Bavaria	6	48
Württemberg	4	17
Saxony	4	23
Baden	3	14
Hesse	3	9

Two other States, Mecklenburg-Schwerin and Brunswick, have each 2 members in the Bundesrath; the former 6 and the latter 3 in the Reichstag; but the remaining 17 States have only 1 each in the Upper House, and none of them more than 3 in the Lower, 11 having only 1 each. Alsace-Lorraine has 4 Commissioners without votes in the Bundesrath, and 15 members in the Reichstag.

The Emperor can only declare war with the consent of the Bundesrath or Federal Council, over which the Chancellor of the Empire presides. He also supervises the Secretaries of State, who are at the head of the principal departments of the government, but do not form a Cabinet. The Ministers are responsible to the Emperor, not to the Legislature. Laws must be passed by the Bundesrath and Reichstag and assented to by the Emperor.

The Imperial Revenue is derived from customs, and certain excise duties, posts, telegraphs, and State railways. To make up any deficiency, the States are assessed in proportion to population. Each of them has its own Provincial Government for local affairs, with legislatures of two Chambers in all the larger ones—the Lower House in Prussia containing 432, and that in Bavaria 156 members.

In the Austro-Hungarian Empire, we have an example of how useful Federation is, in uniting, for purposes of common defence, States whose people are of different races and languages, and who, if independent of each other, would soon fall a prey to some warlike and powerful neighbour. The area of Austria-Hungary would not be too great to be under one Parliament and Executive, if the population were homogeneous; but not being so they require a much larger measure of self-government, to give full scope to their individual ideas. To enjoy this and the safety of the strength of union, the federal system is of vital importance to them.

That mode of government presents itself to us in probably its most complicated form in Austria-Hungary; for this Empire is not only a Confederation, but the first-named portion of it is a Federation—the former term being applied to a union of governments, the latter to a union of states with direct representation of the people.

The Austrian Reichsrath or Parliament consists of an Upper House of 113 members, who are Princes, Nobles, Bishops, and life members nominated by the Emperor for distinguished services rendered in Church or State. To the Lower House of 353 members, Bohemia sends 92, Galicia 63, Lower Austria 37, Moravia 36, Styria 23, Tyrol 18, Upper Austria 17, Küstenland 12, Carniola 10, Silesia 10, Carinthia 9, Bukowina 9, Dalmatia 9, Voralberg 3, and Salzburg 5. The proportion of the representation varies in the Provinces, Galicia having a member to 104,884 inhabitants, and Salzburg to 34,702. All possess Diets, of a single Chamber, for purposes of Provincial self-government.

In Hungary, the Upper House has nearly double the number of members of the Lower, there being besides 286 hereditary and 82 life peers, Archdukes, bishops of the Roman Catholic and Greek Churches, representatives of Protestant Churches and ex-officio members. The Lower House of 453 is elected by voters who are required to have a small qualification. Croatia and Slavonia are represented in both the Hungarian Chambers.

The federal link between federated Austria, and the kingdom of Hungary, is a body of 120, called the Delegations, consisting of 20 members chosen from each of the Upper Houses and 40 from each of the Lower. The Delegations meet annually, alternately at Vienna and Buda-Pesth. The Imperial Ministry is responsible to them. It consists of three Executive departments for the whole Empire. (1) Foreign affairs and those of the Imperial House; (2) War; and (3) Finance. Commercial affairs, indirect taxation, coinage, railways which concern both Austria and Hungary, and defence are also under the control of the Delegations.

There are three budgets, that of the Delegations, that of Austria, and that of Hungary. The expense of common affairs is borne by the two divisions of the Empire, in proportions agreed to, from time to time, by their respective Parliaments, with the sanction of the Emperor. At present the proceeds of the common customs are applied to the purpose, and what more may be required is supplied in the proportion of about 70 per cent. by Austria and 30 per cent. by Hungary.

Switzerland, the smallest of existing federations, is also the oldest of them, having been founded in 1308 by the union of three Cantons. The area of territory, certainly, did not require the application of a form of government which may be abused, if employed merely for the purpose of keeping up a number of small local Parliaments, where one legislature and executive would be sufficient to manage all affairs, both external and internal. It is possible to have too much, as well as too little, machinery of government; and unnecessary Parliaments, Councils, and Boards, mean a greater number of hands put into the pockets of taxpayers.

When the isolated settlements, by means of which New Zealand was occupied, grew together into one Colony, nine Provincial Governments were found to be too much for the country; so one Executive and Parliament was substituted for them, by the will of the people. Here, it may be observed, is a clear example of a Provincial policy with which the rest of the Empire, having no concern, would have had no justification in interfering. The same is true in regard to the division of Queensland, unless the people, not being able to settle the question themselves, appeal to the Imperial authorities to decide for them.

The Swiss Federation, however, grew up when the inhabitants of the country were more completely walled off from each other, by their magnificent mountains, than they are at present; and when a form of government becomes moulded to the traditions and sympathies of a people, no practical men, but only theorists, would root it up. The federal power is centered in a Parliament, composed of a State Council and a National Council, the former of 44 members, two being elected by each of the Cantons. The National Council of 147, represents the whole of Switzerland, at the rate of one member for every 20,000 inhabitants; the five larger Cantons having, Berne 27, Zürich 17, Vaud 12, St. Gall 11, and Aargan 10. There are two with 7, two with 6, five with 5, two with 4, one with 3, three with 2, and two with one member. Every man twenty years of age is entitled to vote. The two Houses are called the Federal Assembly. Laws passed by it may be revised by plebiscite, or *referendum*, as it is called, demanded by 30,000 citizens or eight Cantons. The Executive authority is deputed to the Federal Council of seven members,—elected for three years by the Federal Assembly,—who are ministers of the seven departments of the Government, namely, the Foreign, Home, Justice, Military, Finance and Customs, Agriculture and Industries, Postal and Railways. More than one member from the same Canton cannot be a minister.

The revenue of the Federation is principally derived from customs; there is also a considerable yield from posts and telegraphs. A large portion of the

G

revenue, however, is handed over to the Cantonal Governments. The Federal Government can levy a rate upon the Cantons, according to a scale settled for twenty years.

There is a local government in each of the Cantons— four of the smaller ones having no legislature; but their laws are made, at stated periods, by the people assembled in the open air.

Though an Australian Union has not yet been added to the number of existing Federations, it will probably be so within the next few years, and in a form closely resembling that approved by the Convention in Sydney, in 1891.[1] It will, therefore, be profitable here to note the leading features of the proposed plan—another model, shaped partly from the Canadian and partly from the United States Constitutions, from which to design an Imperial Union.[2]

It provides that the Parliament of " The Commonwealth of Australia " should consist of the Queen, a Senate and House of Representatives. The Queen to appoint a Governor-General; the Senate to be composed by the election of eight members by each Provincial Parliament; the House of Representatives to be elected, for three years, by the electors of the Lower House of each State, in the proportion of one member for every 30,000 people; no State, however, to return less than four. A number of questions is to be taken over by the Federation, but all others are to remain under provincial control. We have here another illustration showing how much greater is the

[1] As to the composition of the Convention, see page 226.
[2] It is given, very clearly and concisely, in Mr. Howard Willoughby's able little work, "Australian Federation," published in Melbourne, in 1891.

demand made by Intercolonial than by Imperial Federation, for the giving up of questions by the Provinces.[1]
By comparing the list in the note below and that in
the one at page 73, with the Imperial questions speci-
fied in next chapter, page 95, we shall see, what a
very few questions need be handed over by the Federal
Governments of Canada and Australia to that of the
Empire. It would really only be essential that certain
general military and naval defences, and strategic
and fortified positions—like King George's Sound,
Halifax, Thursday Island, Esquimault, and Simon's
Bay—should be handed over by the Intercolonial
Federations—as Malta and Gibraltar would be by
England—to be under the Imperial Federal Govern-
ment; certain revenues would also have to be placed

---

[1] The questions are—1. Regulation of trade and commerce. 2.
Customs, excise, and bounties, which shall be uniform, none being
imposed on goods exported from one State to another. 3. Raising
revenue by taxation, which shall be uniform. 4. Borrowing on
federal credit. 5. Posts and telegraphs. 6. Australian military
and naval defence and calling out of forces. 7. Munitions of war.
8. Navigation and shipping. 9. Ocean beacons and buoys, ocean
lighthouses and lightships. 10. Quarantine. 11. Fisheries in
Australian waters beyond territorial limits. 12. Census and
statistics. 13. Currency, coinage, and legal tender. 14. Banks
and issue of paper money. 15. Weights and measures. 16. Bills
and notes. 17. Bankruptcy. 18. Copyrights, patents, designs and
trade marks. 19. Naturalization and aliens. 20. Corporations
foreign or Australian. 21. Marriage and Divorce. 22. Service
and execution of process and judgments of State Courts. 23.
Recognition of laws, acts, records and judicial proceedings of
States. 24. Immigration and emigration. 25. Influx of criminals.
26. Relations with Islands of Pacific. 27. River navigation affecting more than one State. 28. Transport on railways for federal
purposes. 29. Matters upon which any State Parliament may ask
Federal Parliament to legislate for it, other States having the
rights afterwards to adopt the law. 30. Exercise by Federal
Parliament, at request of States concerned, of legislative powers
with respect to Australian territory, now requiring legislation
by Imperial Parliament. 31. Special laws for people of particular
races. 32. Government of territory which may become seat of
Government.

at its disposal.[1] Naturalization should doubtless be under its control. Foreign affairs are so at present, consequently these lists of Canadian and Australian federal questions would be subjected to no substantial subtraction by Imperial Federation ; but its Executive and Parliament would find much work, in managing the great affairs of common concern, and the more numerous smaller matters of general interests, with which the Mother Country has now to deal, and in which the Colonies ought to have a voice.

The proposed Constitution provides that a Supreme Court may be established, but that where public interests are affected, leave may be granted for appeals from it to the Privy Council.

The proposal, so far, to alter the present mode of appointing Provincial Governors by the Crown, as to allow each State to decide as to the mode of appointment of its Governor, was only carried by 20 votes to 19.[2]

The provision that any State Parliament or Parliaments might refer matters for legislation to the Federal Parliament—so that the law might at once affect them, and any other States whose Parliaments might afterwards adopt it—seems to be an original proposal, and it might be found convenient in a Constitution for the Empire.

Mr. Willoughby says—

"The Constitution aims at a true federation of the modern type, inasmuch as it provides for a double count of the people, first as population and then as States. If a nation had been founded, the voting would have been by the people only ; and if a Confederation, the voting would have been by the States alone. Federation is the middle way."

[1] See pages 193, 199–203, 230.   [2] See pages 243–248.

Besides the States, particulars of whose constitutions precede, the Argentine Republic, Mexico, and the new Republic of Brazil, are also federations. These countries, however, have afforded but poor examples of political wisdom. Without referring to them, we can study the system of government we are considering, in a variety of forms—in unions of different sorts and sizes, in Monarchies and Republics, amongst people of several races, creeds, and languages. In all Federalism is a proved success—the making of the greatness of some States—the very life of others.

CHAPTER VI.

POLITICAL ORGANIZATION OF THE EMPIRE.

Six years' rapid development of the Imperial Question—Use and abuse of the word "Imperial"—Federation a well-known form of government—Mr. Forster attaches importance to the discussion of it—Views of the *Times, Australasian,* Mr. Childers, and Sir Julius Vogel—Professor Freeman opposed to Imperial Federation—His definition of Federal government—Questions obviously Imperial; obviously Provincial; and which may be classified under either head. *Imperial Questions*—Defence, Revenue, and expenditure, Foreign affairs, Extensions of the Empire, Government of India and Naturalization—Position of Colonial Office with Imperial Federation. *Provincial Questions*—Church Establishment, Education, Land laws, Taxation and Tariffs, Internal defence, Irish Home Rule, Intercolonial Federation, Alterations of Provincial Constitutions, Native races. *Questions which might be either Imperial or Provincial*—Laws of marriage, domicile, wills, coinage, and copyright, Patent laws, Railways and Telegraphs, Emigration, Final Court of Appeal, Reciprocity—Fiscal policy an open question—How to make England another Holland—*Une puissance finie*—French opinion of British Federation—Napoleon on the "agglomeration" of nations—The Colonies and war—How the United States might have been federated with us—What can separate us?—What do we want to effect Federation?—The question in four sentences—Writ summoning first English Parliament.

On June 14, 1881, at a meeting of the Royal Colonial Institute, over which Sir Alexander Galt presided, I read, as a paper, this chapter, which comes in as a proper sequel to the two which precede—its object being to classify questions Imperial, Provincial, and those which may be treated as either in our federal system. It thus runs with scarcely a change.

Six years ago, on January 19, I had the honour of reading before this Institute, a paper on "The Permanent Unity of the Empire." I was then told by some who differed from me, that I was a theorist, speculating about questions which might be of practical importance to our children or grandchildren, fifty years hence. Such criticism was best left to be disposed of by the march of events; but it could not have been anticipated that, from such various quarters, circumstances should so soon concur, to bring the question of organizing the relations of the different parts of the Empire into such prominence, as to remove it from the region of interesting theories and apparently remote speculations, and, in so short a time, to place it among questions of paramount practical importance. Events have, however, been travelling with that speed which marks all modern progress, but which most conspicuously distinguishes Colonial development. We have had wars; rumours of wars have never been more abundant; anxiety has been so intense, as more than once, to have precluded all hope of the maintenance of peace between our Empire and a great European Power; the nation has passed through days when it had, so to speak, to hold its breath in expectation of hearing the first shot in a conflict, which might have changed the whole aspect of the old continents of Europe and Asia, and have left its traces on the most distant shores of the new continents of America and Australia. Such, briefly, are the circumstances which have, rapidly, invested the question of our Imperial organization with the highest interest, and have proclaimed it to be of vast practical importance.

It is to be regretted that, on the very verge of our

subject, it should be necessary to pause, to enter a
protest against a misappropriation of terms, which is
to be condemned as worse than mere literary piracy.
The word "Imperial"[1]—in its most proper and natural
sense having long been employed by the friends of the
Unity of the Empire, to embrace its largest interests
and greatest policies, in fact all its common concerns—
has recently been taken up by politicians and writers
in the press, to designate what they rightly or wrongly
condemn as an aggressive foreign policy; but into
that point this is neither the time nor place to enter.
Thus, it is attempted to narrow the idea of British
Imperialism, from the broad, noble, pacific sense in
which it has been hitherto understood, and to make
it a synonym for military domination, Cæsarism,
Bonapartism. As long as we call those grand
dominions of which we are all so proud, by the good
old name of the British Empire—which was in use
before the Napoleons and their Imperialism were
thought of—we shall need the adjective "Imperial,"
and to degrade the word, or misapply it to anything
unworthy, should be condemned as most unwise and
unpatriotic.

Having on previous occasions dealt with the subject,[2]
and as time now forbids, I shall not discuss the nature
of the Imperial Constitution, and the modes in which
representation could be extended to all the dominions
of the Empire. It is enough here to observe that
Federal Government is no new idea, no mere theory,
but a practical system, which in some form or other

[1] Let any one who does not like the term "Imperial" Federation
use "British" Federation instead, which is precisely the same
thing. See page 206.
[2] In the two last chapters.

has existed in the world in almost every era within the ken of history;[1] and that to it at the present moment two of the leading nations of the world, the United States of America and the Empire of Germany, owe their position as great Powers. It must, therefore, be a matter of surprise and regret, that among Englishmen—who pride themselves on being above all other people practical, and who may so justly boast that in the past they have always so admirably adapted their government and institutions to the national growth—there should be found those who would counsel us to reject, without trial, a form of government which has created the greatness of other Powers, and which, were it to be successfully applied to the British Empire, would constitute it the greatest Power which has ever appeared amongst the nations of the earth. Is it that the grandeur of a Federated British Empire is beyond the imagination of some minds—that the realization of such a success is something too great to be thought of, too good to be true?

---

[1] It is but little more than eighteen years since Mr. Freeman published, in 1863, the first volume of his very learned "History of Federal Government." At that time, through the apparent break-up of the American Union, that system of government was passing through an almost total eclipse. The historian then said: "Four Federal Commonwealths stand out, in four different ages of the world, as commanding above all others the attention of students of political history." The Governments referred to were the Achæan League, B.C. 281–146; the Swiss Cantons, A.D. 1291–1862; the United Provinces of the Netherlands, A.D. 1579–1795; and the United States of America, A.D. 1778–1862. Mr. Freeman's faith in Federalism—as a means of giving unity and power to peoples of the same race—though evidently strong even in days when the system was under so dark a cloud, could have given him no inkling of the brilliant examples of successful federation, which were so soon to be presented to the world by Germany and the Dominion of Canada. It is to be regretted that, more recently, Professor Freeman has written decidedly against Imperial Federation. Page 206.

FEDERAL BRITAIN.

The splendour of the prospect, instead of condemning, should surely commend Federation to the laudable ambition, to the highest patriotism, to the energies which command success, of every true Briton in England and the Colonies.

It is surely not the part of statesmen to discourage high national aspirations. There is much wisdom in what the Right Hon. W. E. Forster said—in the large and statesmanlike view of Imperial unity which he took in his celebrated address in Edinburgh, in 1875— when he commended the discussion of the idea as the best means of making it "realize itself." Various other weighty opinions may be quoted in favour of keeping the question well before the public.[1] It is a

---

[1] The *Times*, in a leading article of May, 1875, also recognized the great importance of discussing this question. The wisdom of doing so could not be more powerfully urged than in the following words of the article:—

"The Australian Colonies are thoroughly loyal and attached to the Mother Country. . . . The time may come when they will desire to be more closely united with her, and to be admitted to a share in the government of an Empire of which they will be no mean part. . . . The matter may possibly come forward before our own generation has passed away. . . . It may be well that all these matters should be discussed; and there can be at least no harm in the endeavour to familiarize ourselves with the notion of a vast United Empire, in which our remote dependencies in the far-off East and West will find a place, and of which the old country will be the centre and common link of union. For some time yet it can only be a dream; but *it is a dream which we are the better for indulging in, and the day in which it will be fulfilled literally may be nearer than any of us suppose.* It is something meanwhile to be assured that events are proceeding in the right direction. Whatever may be our relations with our Australian Colonies fifty or a hundred years hence, we cannot be wrong now in keeping up a loyal union between all the distant members of the Great Britain that is to be. There can be no possibility of error in such a policy as this." And, the *Times* concludes, this "*may be preparing the way for the grandest Federation of States the world has witnessed.*"

Sir Julius Vogel, in his "Greater or Lesser Britain," in the *Nineteenth Century Review*, July, 1877, remarks that "a very few

pity that Mr. Childers should have adopted a tone of
discouragement, at so early a stage of the consideration

ardent men who long for Confederation, believe it possible; " and
that as " the vast body of the people, whose minds are now colour-
less on the question, are favourably predisposed to retaining the
Colonies, there is good material to work on, if the case be vigorously
taken up. Given those who are willing to become advocates of
the cause, they will find multitudes willing to follow them, and
large as their object is, they may reduce it to the simple proposition
—that it is the duty of the Mother Country to declare that she
holds, and will hold, the Colonies as part of her territories, that
through the Empire the people must grow up in that belief, and
must shape their legislation, their institutions, and their aspirations accordingly." . . . " The question whether Confederation is
desirable is another way of asking if it is desirable to retain the
Colonies."

The *Australasian*, in a leading article on July 10, 1880, on
" The Consolidation of the Empire," says : Whenever the Imperial
Parliament is remodelled, as remodelled it surely will be, either
by its own deliberate act or by its signal breakdown, under the
intolerable multiplicity and magnitude of the functions it has to
perform, and when it disencumbers itself of the merely municipal
and parish vestry business which now occupies so much of its
time and attention, we may reasonably expect that it will take
an entirely Imperial view of its august duties and responsibilities,
and attend exclusively to Imperial interest and concerns. In that
event, the consolidation of the Empire will be one of the foremost
achievements to be aimed at by any Ministry, ambitious of making
for itself an immortal name by welding together into one grand
unity the huge but unarticulated joints and members of that
which will become in deed as well as in name the British Empire.
But, inasmuch as the initiative of nearly all great schemes of
policy and beneficial reforms has been taken outside of the
Administration for the time being, and public opinion, enlightened
and clarified by protracted discussion and exhaustive controversy,
has first matured those changes, and then insisted upon their
being carried into effect; so, too, in regard to this question of the
consolidation of the Empire : its continued agitation and earnest
debate must precede, and will be of great advantage to, its
eventual settlement. And for this reason we are glad to see that
the relations of Great Britain to her Colonies are occupying the
attention of the Colonial Institute in London, and to learn that
the Duke of Manchester, the President of that Institute, and a
warm friend of the movement, is about to visit these Colonies,
when he will have an opportunity of conversing with our leading
public men upon the subject, and of judging for himself of the
importance of linking the Australian dependencies of the Crown
with 'cables of perturbable toughness.' Colonists who are residing

of the question.[1] The right hon. gentleman is reported
to have said : " I deprecate and reject all those fanciful
notions of bringing the United Kingdom and her
Colonies and dependencies into a Bund, or Zollverein,
or some such combination, with a Federal Parliament,
which have caught so many well-meaning people of
late years, and at which Lord Beaconsfield hinted
himself in one of his speeches in the North. If you

in or are ou a visit to England, ought to be able to contribute to
the discussions of the Institute many useful suggestions with
respect to the best method of bringing about the substantial
incorporation of the extremities of the Empire with its head and
heart ; and although the ancillary question of a federation of this
group of Colonies is a highly important one, it is secondary to the
much larger one of the Imperial consolidation. That this would
be compatible with the enjoyment and exercise of the same powers
of self-government as those which have been conferred upon us by
the Imperial Parliament, it is almost superfluous to insist upon.
No resident in Oregon, or Florida, or Decotah, or New Mexico,
feels his liberty or his political independence is in the slightest
degree impaired because a Federal Congress, meeting in a city
some hundreds or thousands of miles distant from his State, enacts
certain laws which are binding upon the people of the whole Union,
and imposes certain taxes which have to be paid by every citizen
of the Republic. Americans are justly proud of belonging to a
Political Confederation which embraces something like 45,000,000
of people, occupying a territory of 3,600,000 square miles. . . .
Great Britain and her dependencies comprise an area of 4,677,432
square miles, peopled by upwards of 200,000,000 inhabitants, and
embracing every variety of soil and climate. There is an Empire,
such as Alexander never contemplated and Rome never attained
to. . . . United, they would be invulnerable and irresistible, and as
they are especially devoted to the arts of peace and industry, their
predominating influence in the affairs of the world would be
exerted on behalf of commerce and civilization. But, loosely
connected as the British dominions now are, their power and
prestige suffer materially from the want of union and consolidation.
. . . If the Empire were consolidated, a truly Imperial Parliament,
representative of the whole of its constituent portions, would
provide for the defence of every member of it, with Imperial
means, on an Imperial scale of magnitude.

The *Australasian* strongly adhered to this policy, for on
January 3, 1885, it had an article warmly supporting the Imperial
Federation League and its objects.

[1] Speech at Pontefract, October 16, 1879.

want to find a good cause of quarrel with your Colonies
this would be the method, and I speak with some
little knowledge of Colonial politics." In a subsequent
speech, Mr. Childers declared himself to be strongly
in favour of maintaining the union with the Colonies,
and of defending them even to the extent of keeping
up a navy equal to that of three other Powers
combined;[1] but he did not say whether the Colonies
should contribute anything towards its support, or
ever be allowed any voice in a foreign policy which
might involve them in wars. He had no suggestion
to make as to any Imperial organization. The right
hon. gentleman relied much upon his Colonial
knowledge. He certainly knew, Victoria, more than
a quarter of a century ago, when he was a member of
her first Legislature, and afterwards of her first
responsible Ministry, but he has since had much to
absorb his attention in other directions. He cannot
therefore imagine the infant Colony of his former
recollections, becoming one of the United Provinces
of a British Federation. There is one thing above all
others which Colonial knowledge teaches—and Mr.
Childers, doubtless, had no intention to act contrary
to it—and that is, that no man, in this country,
should venture to speak, unless specially delegated
to do so, as if he were an accredited exponent of
Colonial opinion, or the spokesman of any particular
Colony. Arguing, however, as any one may do, from
Colonial knowledge and experience, it is safe to assert
that the Colonies are capable of appreciating grand
conceptions, and of carrying out great enterprises and
policies, and that no policy to which they can aspire

---

[1] Mr. Childers's foresight has been borne out by facts up to the
latest date.

can bo greater, more beneficial to their interests or
conducive to their fame, than the policy of Imperial
Federation.

Whatever may be the future relations of the different
parts of the British Empire to each other—whether a
Bund, or Zollverein, or Federal Parliament and Executive be established—or even if it should be possible, as
Mr. Childers imagines, for the Colonies, after they
have passed further away from their days of infancy,
to remain united to England, with no form of Imperial
government more perfectly organized than that which
at present exists—it would still be necessary to draw a
clear distinction between questions of Imperial importance, and those which are purely Provincial, or only of
inter-Provincial concern.

The purpose of this paper is to attempt to some
extent to classify such questions; and when we come
to consider them, it is not so difficult to assign them
their proper places. We have so much practical experience of Federal Government in Switzerland, in
Germany, in the United States, in Canada, that we
can soon understand what questions must of necessity
be Imperial in the Federation of Great Britain.[1] In
fact, it will be easier for us to distinguish such questions, than if all the dominions of the Empire were as
contiguous as those of the Federal Governments referred to.[2] The distinction, which it is most important

[1] See pages 73–84.
[2] The following is Mr. Freeman's valuable definition: "The
name of Federal Government may, in its widest sense, be applied
to any union of component members where the degree of union
between the members surpasses that of mere alliance, however
intimate, and where the degree of independence possessed by each
member surpasses anything which can fairly come under the head
of merely municipal freedom. . . . Two requisites seem necessary
to constitute a Federal Government in its most perfect form. On

to keep in view, will most clearly appear if we set down—

First:[1] questions which are obviously Imperial, or of common concern;

Second: those which are obviously Provincial; and

Third: those which may be left either to the control of the Imperial Government or of the Provincial Governments.

I.—IMPERIAL QUESTIONS.

Defence.—The first and most important purpose for which all Governments exist, is the defence of nations

the one hand, each of the members of the Union must be wholly independent in those matters which concern each member only. On the other hand, all must be subject to the common power in those matters which concern the whole body of members collectively. Thus each member will fix for itself the laws of its criminal jurisprudence, and even the details of its political constitution. And it will do this, not as a matter of privilege or concession from any higher power, but as a matter of absolute right, by virtue of its inherent powers as an independent commonwealth. But in all matters which concern the general body, the sovereignty of the several members will cease. Each member is perfectly independent within its own sphere, but there is another sphere in which its independence, or rather its separate existence, vanishes. It is invested with every right of sovereignty on one class of subjects, but there is another class of subjects on which it is as incapable of separate political action as any province or city of a monarchy or of an indivisible republic. The making of peace and war, the sending and receiving of ambassadors, generally all that comes within the department of International Law, will be reserved wholly to the central power. Indeed, the very existence of the several members of the Union will be diplomatically unknown to foreign nations, which will never be called upon to deal with any power except the central government. A Federal Union, in short, will form one State in relation to other powers, but many States as regards its internal administration. This complete division of sovereignty we may look upon as essential to the absolute perfection of the Federal idea.'' See distinction between Federation and Confederation, pages 64, 70, 78, 84.

[1] How small would be the demand made by Imperial Federation, and how extensive by Intercolonial Federation, upon the Provinces for control of questions, will be seen by reference to lists of Canadian and Australian Federal questions at pages 73 and 83.

against the attacks of external foes. The more powerful the nation, the more secure must be all its territories against such attacks. The United Kingdom,
Canada, Australia, South Africa, standing alone might
be subdued; united in a firm bond of defence they
must in the future be invincible, if not invulnerable.
What foreign Power would, a century or half a century
hence, think of attacking them if they should be
thoroughly united and organized? The only hope
for the enemies of their nationality would be to sow
division among them, with a view of vanquishing in
detail the shattered portions of the disintegrated
Empire, or perhaps of appropriating some fragments
of the wreck. It is, therefore, obvious that—unless
some great injury to their individual prosperity must
result from their remaining permanently united—these
great British countries should ever consider themselves
as forming but one indissoluble nation, and should
combine their defences. Far from their provincial
interests being injuriously affected by such co-operation, they would be greatly benefited. Each province,
instead of having to bear single-handed the entire
burden of its own defence, would be comparatively
unconscious that it had anything to contribute. Its
perfect security, in the united strength of the Empire,
would enable it to devote its energies, without dread
or danger, to the peaceful development of its own
prosperity.

The organization of the defences of the Empire is
therefore the most important question of common
concern; it is already of great and growing practical
importance. Recent alarms of war have shown it to
be urgent. It is not enough that Mother Country and
Colonies should vie with each other in devotion to the

principle of unity which binds them together. National sentiment is a mighty power, but it must take some tangible practical shape; it must gather up the strength of a people; it must organize their resources for defence, if it is to be effective, if it is to be anything more than a name. All the defences of the Empire, over and above those required for the purposes of mere provincial police, should be organized upon a uniform and comprehensive Imperial system. All the land and sea forces of the Empire should be maintained with a view of rendering the most effective protection to all our dominions. Captain Colomb, in so ably pointing out before this Institute and elsewhere, the steps which should be taken to defend our Empire, has also done invaluable service in proving the practical nature of the questions of Imperial organization and Federation. He has pointed out how the great highways of our Empire should be guarded; how all our dominions are equally interested in the question; what strength and security they would derive from co-operative defence; and what great resources they could contribute for the purpose. Details cannot be discussed within the limits of such a chapter as this, but leading outlines may be given. The Imperial authorities, representing the whole Empire, would have to decide upon the positions of naval and coaling stations, the strength of the Imperial army and navy, the centres where they should be concentrated, the mode in which they should co-operate with provincial militias and volunteer forces. Naval and military schools, and colleges would also eventually have to be established in different parts of the Empire; and, although the Imperial army would be small, it would be desirable to afford to the youth for whom in all parts of the world a soldier's life has attractions, opportunities of entering the Imperial service. Thus, the roll of the British drum would once more be heard following the sun round the globe; and the red coat, which ought never to have been altogether withdrawn from the eyes of Colonial-born Britons, would again be presented to their view. The presence of some regular troops in different parts of the Empire, would also be important, for the purpose of furnishing a standard of efficiency to provincial militias and volunteers.[1]

A greater navy than that which Mr. Childers contemplates would also soon spring up, if organized on an Imperial basis, without the United Kingdom or any other part of the Empire feeling it to be a burden. It would be sufficient to protect all our coasts, our ocean highways, and our commerce; for with the increasing numbers of our ships and sailors,—the growth of our Colonies and commerce,—it is no extravagant expectation that such an Imperial navy would grow up, as to render it impossible for any enemy's war-ships to live upon the ocean.

Revenue and Expenditure.—Joint defence must be at joint expense. Each portion of the Empire would have to contribute its fair share of the Imperial revenue, and would be entitled to a voice in its expenditure. Constitutional government justly provides that there shall be no taxation without representation. Therefore, this practical, urgent question of defence, is inseparable from the practical question of ways and means, which, in its turn, is as indissolubly linked to the question of representation. Thus, by the irresistible and most practical logic of facts,

[1] See Appendix, page 253.

are we brought face to face with the Imperial question of Federation. It would be for the representatives of the whole Empire to decide what taxes should be levied, to raise a revenue to maintain our defences and to meet all other Imperial expenditure. Our present object being to indicate what are Imperial and what are non-Imperial questions; to enter into details, after ascertaining the class to which a particular question belongs, would be superfluous if not irrelevant. These details have been worked out under existing systems of Federal Government.[1] They have not unfrequently been discussed in connection with the subject of federating our British Empire. My friend Mr. Frederick Young, in his able letters to *The Colonies* newspaper, reprinted in a valuable volume entitled, "Imperial Federation," has conclusively shown how futile it is to attempt to set up barriers of petty details against the adoption of this great policy. It is only necessary here to remark, that a complete Imperial Government should have direct power to levy taxes, and not merely to impose subsidies upon the various Provincial Governments of the Empire;[2] and that the revenue should be raised in the easiest and simplest ways, interfering as little as possible with commerce and with Provincial fiscal arrangements. With the growth of wealth and population throughout our vast dominions, the percentage of Imperial revenue required would decline. It would always be much less than what each province would have to provide for its own defence if, instead of co-operating with the others, it were in the much weaker and more heavily burdened position of independence.

Foreign Affairs.[3]—Given a system of joint defence, it

---

[1] See pages 72–85.　　[2] See pages 193, 200.　　[3] Pages 159, 180.

follows as a natural consequence that all those who
help to maintain it should have a voice in conducting
those foreign relations, which alone render national
defence a necessity. Nay, it is but just that those
who are exposed to a common danger should be heard
respecting affairs which may lead to such danger, even
though they may have but little strength to aid in
the defence. Joint defence at joint expense entitles
to joint control of external affairs. This should be as
well-recognized a maxim of our British Imperial union,
as the well-known constitutional one about taxation
and representation going together. All treaties and
negotiations with foreign nations should be conducted
through an Imperial administration responsible to· a
Parliament, in which every portion of the Empire
should have its fair share of representation. One
great change for the better would certainly be brought
about, by having a distinct Federal Ministry for Imperial purposes. Foreign affairs would cease to be a
bone of contention between the political parties of this
country, and a stalking-horse upon which they too
often try to win the race for power. Foreign policy,
instead of being thus mixed up with Provincial party
struggles, would be removed to a broader and calmer
sphere, where it would be solely considered upon its
own merits as affecting the Empire at large. There
is no other escape from its continuing to be bound up,
as part and parcel, with questions with which it has
nothing whatever to do—the purely domestic politics
of the British Isles—and being viewed from the least
elevated party standpoints, except by being lifted into
the larger and higher sphere of Imperial Federal
questions.

Extensions of the Empire.—These should be made by

the Imperial Government, the new territories being in the first instance under its immediate control, as Crown Colonies are at present; but afterwards they could be attached to the nearest province of the Empire, or, on becoming of sufficient importance, should be invested with all the powers of Provincial self-government. Thus, for example, fresh territories like those newly acquired in Africa, would at first be under direct Imperial control. If, however, there existed an adjacent Colony, or Intercolonial Federation, of sufficient strength to govern them, these territories would naturally be incorporated with the Colony, or, on acquiring a sufficiently large European population, would have Provincial self-government conferred upon them, and be included in the Intercolonial Federation. From the correspondence laid before Parliament in 1876, it is clear that Eastern New Guinea would have been annexed, had the Australian Colonies responded to Lord Carnarvon's suggestion that they should contribute to the expense. They did not do so because they would have had no control in the management of a territory, of which the cost of government would have been partly borne by them; and the Colonial Office, considering that Australia was primarily interested in New Guinea, was not prepared to effect the annexation at the sole cost of the Mother Country. No more striking illustration could be given of the want of Imperial organization. A territory, acknowledged to be of value to the Mother Country and the Colonies, could not be acquired, because the imperfection of our existing system would not admit of the question of cost and control being properly adjusted between England and Australia.

India.—The great Oriental Empire would present no obstacle to the complete organized union of the British nation in England and the Colonies. Without in the least underrating the value of India, there is no doubt that its possession has hitherto been esteemed in this country out of proportion to its worth as compared with the Colonies. The dependent Empire has been of immense advantage, in bringing wealth to these Isles, and in the training of British soldiers and statesmen; but the people of India have derived much greater benefits from us than we have from them. History will for ever record what the just rule, and splendid administration, of Britain have done for the subject races of the East, who first experienced from their conquerors the blessings of peace and justice, and of freedom from cruelty and oppression. But, though war and disaster have befallen England on account of India, and may befall her again, and though India involves the most serious problems of foreign policy, some who would have England endure everything for her, have objected to the, really and comparatively, light risks and responsibilities which the Mother Country may incur from the Colonial Empire. Seeing how India is esteemed in this country, it is possible that were a Federation of the Empire to be formed, some people might wish to keep India under the control of the Parliament and Executive of the British Isles. But even if such an arrangement could be carried out, it would be much better for the Mother Country to share the advantages, as well as the risks and burdens, of governing India with her partners in the Empire, than retain both herself. India handed over to the Federal Government would be held with a firmer grasp, which would strengthen with the growing wealth, population, and power of the Colonial dominions. If foreign affairs were placed under an Imperial Government, and India left to the Government of the United Kingdom, serious difficulties might arise in conducting relations with other Powers. The Federal Empire would doubtless not be less alive to its great responsibilities with respect to India, or indifferent to any of the British obligations contracted with regard to that country, and would be fully sensible of the prestige arising from its possession. Some means might perhaps also ultimately be devised for giving India representation in the Federal Parliament.

Naturalization.—The conditions upon which foreigners should be admitted to British citizenship, must always be regulated by Imperial authority.

Other minor Imperial questions might be enumerated, but they would all come under the cardinal headings already given, namely, Defence, Imperial Revenue and Expenditure, Foreign Affairs, Extensions of the Empire, and Government of India. With a Federal organization there would be no longer a Colonial Office; for the business of that department would properly belong to the Imperial Prime Minister, who, unless he might also happen to be head of the English Cabinet, would not be occupied with the provincial affairs of the United Kingdom. He would exercise a general supervision over the common concerns of the Empire, and would have in his gift the appointment of Provincial governors, and all other Imperial patronage within the Empire.

II.—PROVINCIAL QUESTIONS.

It is essential to the right understanding of Imperial organization or Federation, that we should fully bear in mind what questions are obviously Provincial, and which must therefore on no account be interfered with by any Federal authority. From want of due consideration of this point, many people have hastily condemned the proposal that the Colonies should send Federal representatives to this country. It has been erroneously assumed that these Colonial members would sit in the Parliament, and have a voice in all the domestic questions of the United Kingdom—an arrangement which would be highly unfair and objectionable. Colonial representatives should come to England for Imperial purposes alone, and to sit, not in the Parliament of England, Wales, Scotland, and Ireland, but in a distinct Imperial Parliament of the whole Empire of Great Britain. This legislature would take over all the questions of common concern to the Empire, and would leave full and exclusive control of the affairs of the United Kingdom to the insular Parliament; which would then be enabled to devote to them the amount of attention they demand, but which from present pressure of business it cannot afford to bestow upon them.

It will only be necessary to mention some of these Provincial questions to show at once that they must always remain in their present category. Many of them excite strong party feelings, but it is not in the least necessary, for the purpose of distinguishing between them and Imperial questions, that we should give any consideration to their merits, or indicate that we take one side rather than another with respect to them.

Church Establishment.—This question is obviously one for the consideration of the people of the United Kingdom. Representatives of other parts of the

Empire, brought to England for Imperial purposes, would therefore not have the remotest claim to interfere in any way with it; and the terms of the Federal Constitution would of course expressly prevent them from touching such a question.

Education, again, should be left to the exclusive control of the governments of the provinces of the Empire, so that whatever systems might be best adapted to the wants, opinions, and circumstances of their respective populations should be carried out. To this rule there might be one exception. It would be desirable, though not essential to our Imperial organization, that the highest educational institutions —the universities of the Empire—should be of Imperial creation. This does not imply that they should not be placed under the control of the Provincial governments, but that they should have the stamp of Imperial recognition. Oxford, Cambridge, and the other universities of these Kingdoms, would not be handed over to the control of the Parliament of the Empire, but would remain subject to that of this country.

Land Laws.—The regulation of the holding, disposal of, and succession to the lands of any country is of great importance to the inhabitants, but can only be of remote interest to people living at a distance. It was wise of the Mother Country, in conferring self-government upon the Colonies, to give them the control of the waste lands, although much may be said in favour of the idea that a portion of the revenue arising from Colonial land sales, should have been reserved for the purposes of promoting emigration from the United Kingdom. It is certain that the disposal of the lands in the Colonies could not have been managed as well from Downing Street, as by means of even the least satisfactory arrangements for the purpose made on the spot by Colonial Governments. Provincial land questions can, therefore, in no way affect Imperial relations. The unity of the Empire would be no stronger, if it were possible to have uniform land laws through its entire territories ; nor would it be weaker by having the most widely different systems—primogeniture and strict entails in some of the British dominions, and the most opposite system, the French law of succession, in others. Land tenure in England, Scotland, and Ireland would, therefore, be regulated by the legislature of these Kingdoms, even if the most complete Federal Parliament of the Empire held its sittings in this country ; and in like manner the Provincial Legislatures of the Colonies would, without Imperial Federal control, regulate their land systems.

Taxation and Tariffs.—The control of the Provincial Legislatures over the fiscal arrangements of their respective territories, need in no way be affected by the limited taxation which the Imperial Parliament might be empowered to impose, in order to raise ample revenues for Federal purposes. It has been already intimated that it would be the policy of that Parliament to levy taxes in the simplest and most convenient form, having regard to all interests concerned. There would not be the least necessity for restricting the liberty now enjoyed by each Colony, of adopting such tariffs as it at present, rightly or wrongly, considers most suited to its own interests. Were a Federal Government established, there would be no more reason than at present why Victoria, with her high protectionist policy, should not remain in the Empire, and be an important element of strength in its federated union.

The only restrictions upon the power of the Provincial Parliaments, as to fiscal policy, would be those already existing, which prevent differential duties from being levied in such a manner as to admit foreign imports, on more favourable terms than may be extended to those from other territories of the Empire. By Act of the Imperial Parliament the Australian Colonies are now allowed to adopt differential duties in each other's favour. Of course, it would be desirable that all portions of the Empire could see their way to the adoption of the same fiscal policy ; but it is not essential to their co-operating for common purposes.

Internal Defence.—As the Federal Government would have to provide for the defence of all the territories of the Empire against external attack, so the Provincial Governments would have to maintain peace and order within their respective limits. As the Colonies grow in strength and population, they will cease to require that aid in native wars which has hitherto been indispensable to the existence of some of them. New Zealand will never again require that assistance which she received from the Mother Country in her early days, and without which her infant growth might have been stunted or cut short. We should merit the contempt of the civilized world, were we to leave our 30,000 countrymen in Natal to the mercy of the native population, which so greatly outnumbers them both within and without the limits of the Colony. When the present troubles [1] are settled in South Africa, and the Colonies there are strengthened by a large increase of British population, native difficulties will become purely Provincial questions, requiring no Imperial intervention. The Federal authorities would, there-

[1] This was in 1881.

fore, have nothing to do with Provincial defences, except to aid in promoting their efficiency, by enabling local forces to have as much benefit as possible from the instruction of such regular Imperial troops as might happen to be stationed in different parts of the Empire.[1]   Colonial militias, like the English militia, might volunteer for external service in time of war; and in the event of the invasion of any of our territories, it would be necessary that the Imperial Government should take the entire command of the Provincial forces of such territories.

Irish Home Rule, which solely relates to the good government of these Isles, should be left exclusively to be dealt with by their inhabitants.   Such a question shows how unwise, and unnecessary, it would be for a Parliament of the Empire to interfere with Provincial affairs.   There would be no reason for its doing so; and no friend of Federal Government would wish to see it entrusted with any power over questions not of general Imperial concern.   Home Rule, whether it come to nothing or lead to some change in the relations of Ireland to the United Kingdom, can neither facilitate nor impede the progress of the much larger, and more important, question of the organization or federation of the United Empire; and the subject can have no interest for our countrymen beyond the British Isles, save in so far as they always heartily desire, that every domestic question may be settled in a manner most conducive to the best interests of these old parent lands.

Intercolonial Federation.—This, again, is a question more for Provincial than for Imperial consideration.   Only under such circumstances as those which at present[2]

---

[1] See Appendix, 253.   [2] In 1881.

exist in South Africa, could any claim to a voice in the settlement of such a question be urged from without. If any colonies require external aid for protection against internal dangers, the Imperial Government coming to their assistance, certainly establishes a right to be heard, in recommending to the colonists federation, or any other kind of co-operation, for the purposes of more effective internal defence. To Colonies circumstanced like those of Australia, Intercolonial Federation is simply a question of the most convenient arrangement of their common Provincial affairs between themselves. It is, therefore, for them, and them only, to decide whether they will ever adopt it. Should they do so, an Imperial Act would be required for the purpose, but that would be passed with even less difficulty than was presented in the case of Canada; for the Federation of that Dominion involved some important points of Imperial concern, arising out of the proximity of the United States.

Alterations of Provincial Constitutions.—It can only be in exceptional instances, that changes in Provincial constitutions can directly affect interests, beyond the limits of the Dominions or Colonies governed by such constitutions. These enactments provide that they cannot be changed in certain particulars, by the Colonial Parliaments, without the amending acts being reserved for the sanction of the Imperial Government. With a Federated Empire this requirement would be as essential as at present; so that there should be no chance of Imperial rights being affected by the constitutions of Provinces being altered, without the Imperial authorities having an opportunity of supervising what was being done. Practically, however, judging from experience since self-government has been set up in the Colonies, a veto upon measures of colonial constitutional reform passed by Provincial legislatures, would be seldom or never exercised. Were the Canadian Parliament, for instance, to follow the recent example of New Zealand, and to abolish, with their consent, all the Provincial Governments, centering all legislative power in the Dominion Parliament, such a change, if referred to the Imperial authorities, would as a matter of course be sanctioned. Then, again, upon purely Provincial grounds, it would be desirable that differences between Provinces or between the branches of their respective legislatures, should, when all other means of removing them had been exhausted, be referred to the conciliatory mediation, arbitration, or legislative intervention of the Imperial Government. With a Federation of the Empire, the only difference with respect to Mr. Graham Berry's recent mission would have been, that the negotiations would have been carried on with the Federal Prime Minister, instead of the Secretary of State for the Colonies—a minister who would not exist; and some member for Victoria might have brought the question of the revision of the constitution of the Colony before the Federal Parliament; but probably without resulting in any departure from the policy of non-interference wisely laid down by Sir Michael Hicks-Beach.

Native Races.—I would now add to the list given when the paper was produced, the question of dealing with native races, which should be left to Intercolonial Federations or Provincial Governments, who alone, from local knowledge, are fitted to deal with them; and our countrymen in the Colonies are as much to be trusted, to act justly and humanly, as those of them who inhabit the British Isles.

III.—QUESTIONS WHICH MIGHT BE LEFT EITHER TO THE
IMPERIAL OR PROVINCIAL GOVERNMENTS.[1]

Our classification would be very incomplete if mention
were not made of some questions of which the control
may, without impairing the strength or efficiency of
the Imperial organization, be left either to the Federal
or Provincial Governments.

The Laws of Marriage will, perhaps, furnish the best
illustration of this class of questions. Everybody will
admit that it would be very desirable that these laws
should be uniform in England, Scotland, and Ireland.
But they cannot easily be made so. Their difference,
however, has never been a source of political weakness
to the United Kingdom, and would be less so to the
United Empire, although the legalization of marriage
with a deceased wife's sister in the Colonies has created
a fresh distinction. The best and most convenient,
though by no means indispensable arrangement, would
be that the laws of marriage should be regulated by
the Federal Parliament for the whole Empire.

Domicile.—With differences of marriage law, and
also with respect to succession to property, it must
be all the more important that the law of domicile
should be as clear as possible; for the legality of a
marriage, and questions respecting the succession to
property, may turn upon the domicile of particular
persons. We are familiar with the popular expression,
" the glorious uncertainty of the law ;" but it is as
often the glorious uncertainty of the facts, to which
the clearest law has to be applied, which occasions the

---

[1] See page 84 as to mode of referring questions for legislation,
by Provincial Parliaments to that of Federation, devised by
Australian Convention. These might be so dealt with.

cost, delays, and disappointments of litigation. For instance, it depends upon a fact, often most uncertain —the intention of a colonist, dying in this country, to make his abode in England or to return to his Colony,—whether his personal estate in the Colonies shall pay legacy duty to the Exchequer here, in addition to what may be charged upon it by the Colonial Government. It would, therefore, be desirable to have the incidents of domicile made as simple and uniform as possible throughout the Empire; and that could be better arranged by the Imperial Government than by the different Provincial Governments.

Wills.—As a matter of convenience and a means of avoiding serious mistakes, it is desirable that British people, so many of whom are constantly moving about through the Empire, should have only one simple mode of making and executing wills. All legislation upon this subject may, therefore, be best entrusted to an Imperial Parliament.

Coinage, Copyright, and Patent Laws, though in no way affecting the unity of the Empire, could also be most conveniently regulated by Federal legislation.

Railways, Steamers, and Telegraphs.—The construction of means of communication for the opening up of their own territories, must primarily be of Provincial or Inter-Provincial importance, and should therefore be left to the control of the Provincial Governments. There may, however, be one or two main lines of railways of such consequence as to be of Imperial interest. For instance, a line, like the Canadian Pacific Railway, might be regarded as of such Imperial importance, as to induce a Federal Parliament to hasten its construction by means of a guarantee. Lines of telegraph and of mail steamers, connecting the different dominions of the Empire would, however, more frequently call for Imperial subsidies, especially if the wise arrangement be made, to have vessels constructed so as to be available as cruisers in the event of war.

Emigration might, perhaps, under any system of Imperial organization, remain a question between this over-peopled country, and such of the Colonies as appreciate the fact that population is one of their greatest wants. Imperial Federation, however,—with the enlarged ideas and feelings which it could not fail to impress upon our people,—would make them regard themselves, whether in England, Canada, South Africa, or Australia, as but one nation. This conviction ought to convince them that in order to develop, and fertilize our splendid new lands, as well as to enrich their sparse inhabitants, those vast territories should be irrigated by a steady stream of people, from the overflowing human reservoir pent up in these old countries. One of the truest policies for building up the Empire would be to put its waste people upon its waste lands.

Final Court of Appeal.—Under the existing organization of the Empire, it is an undoubted advantage to the Colonies to have the right of appeal to the Judicial Committee of the Privy Council; and this is so much appreciated that the Dominion Act, though establishing a Final Court of Appeal for Canada, provides that either party to a suit, may require that it shall be carried from the inferior Courts to the Privy Council, instead of to the Dominion Court of Final Appeal. With Imperial Federation it would certainly be necessary that, at least in all cases affecting Imperial rights, there should be an appeal to the highest divisions of the Imperial Court in the Metropolis of the Empire, even if branches of that Court were established in the Colonies. The inhabitants of the Provinces would probably always desire to retain the privilege of final appeal, even in private litigation, to such a great tribunal as would be composed of the most eminent judges, who could be gathered from among the ablest lawyers, and greatest judicial intellects which the British dominions would produce.

Reciprocity.—We have already seen that Imperial Federation need not interfere with Provincial fiscal policies, and that as long as differential duties are only adopted as a matter of convenience between Provinces of the Empire with adjacent territories, the Provincial Parliaments may well be left to arrange their own tariffs. It may, however, be felt throughout the Empire that it would be of great advantage to come to some reciprocal arrangement respecting an Imperial commercial policy. It is probable that our various dominions may never think alike on the great and difficult politico-economical questions of Free Trade and Protection. England has tried hard to convert other nations to that great policy which has for a time, if not permanently, given such an impulse to her prosperity. But she has tried in vain; and never did success seem less likely to reward her efforts than at the present moment. It might, therefore, be worth her consideration, whether she may not yet do within her own Empire what she cannot do outside it. For the sake of the greater extension of Free Trade in the world, she might find it wise to abandon or modify that policy, as regards foreign countries which so resolutely oppose it, if by so doing she could promote its adoption throughout her Empire. She might thus bring a far greater surface of the globe within that policy than she can do by efforts, which now seem almost Quixotic, to induce her foreign neighbours to adopt it. The United States, though Protectionist as to the outside world, are within themselves the greatest Free Trade territory upon earth. Might not the United Empire of Great Britain excel them also in this? Had England, instead of attempting to make foreigners Free-traders, turned her attention to her own Empire, she might perhaps by this time have carried Free Trade much further. She might, in their interests as well as her own, have held out inducements which would have prevented her Colonies from adopting Protection against her and against each other. For instance, if she had admitted Canadian and other Colonial grain and raw materials free into the United Kingdom, whilst retaining a duty upon those from Russia and the United States, on condition that the Colonies should tax foreign manufactures, what might have been the effect? Hundreds of thousands of British people who have gone to the United States, and enabled manufactures to be created there as rivals to those of England, would have settled in Canada and other British territories, and would have opened lands, which still remain untilled, in order to produce food for the Mother Country, whose manufactures would in return have been taken by the colonists; and thus Free Trade, which does not exist on the part of some of the chief Colonies towards the Mother Country, might have been established between them. As the trade of England with her own empire will so soon leave her foreign trade far behind, and as the trade of so extensive an empire will probably be chiefly within its own limits, it would be desirable that our commercial relations should become as unrestricted as possible.

It would be the greatest triumph for Free Trade, short of universal adoption amongst all nations, to be extended throughout the length and breadth of the Empire of Great Britain. It is now only possible to indicate, without attempting to discuss it, a question which may become of great interest to the whole United Empire, and which may possibly be adopted by it as an Imperial policy. It is satisfactory, however, without having to explore the merits or demerits of Imperial Reciprocity, to be able to see that it need not be adopted unless it commend itself to the people of the Empire at large. However they may regard it, for the sake of its convenience and commercial advantages, it cannot be essential to their unity, for purposes of common strength and protection. The more, however, they feel that they are one people, one nation, and that their most distant territories are but parts of a common Fatherland, the more will they be disposed to regard their interests as identical, and to promote the most unrestricted trade among themselves.

Without some organization of the great and growing defensive strength and resources of the Colonies with those of these Isles, there may seem to be some justification for the contracted estimate of British power, in Mr. Gladstone's Midlothian speech of November 25th, 1879, as reported in the *Times:* " I wish to dissipate, if I can, the idle dreams of those who are always telling you that the strength of England depends, sometimes they say upon its prestige, sometimes upon its extending its Empire, and upon what it possesses beyond these shores. Rely upon it, the strength of Great Britain and Ireland is within the United Kingdom. Whatever . . . is to be done must be done by the force derived from you and from your children—derived from you and your fellow-electors in the land; from you and the citizens and people of this country." Let us slightly alter the words of the statesman, and see if we cannot produce something more logical and forcible. " Rely upon it, the strength of Holland is within the Netherlands." But shall we stop here; shall we not draw the inevitable conclusion? If Holland, in the days of her fame and greatness, could have extended herself, could have acquired and consolidated with herself large Colonial dominions peopled by her own race, she might now hold rank among the Great Powers of Europe. So if England, disregarding narrow insular counsels, have but the wisdom to weld, and organize with herself in indissoluble union, her great Colonial possessions, she will in the future command a strength tenfold as great as she can ever alone possess, and there will be no fear of the history of Holland being repeated with respect to her; no danger of the growth of other nations, with which her narrow limits, and already teeming population, must preclude her from keeping pace, leaving her far behind, and eventually causing her to be dropped out of the list of Great Powers.

Prince Bismarck is reported to have once said—but it is incredible that the great statesman could have seriously expressed such an opinion—that England was "*une puissance finie.*" Should England, enervated by wealth and luxury, come to regard her manufactures, her commerce, her money-making, as everything, and national spirit and feeling as nothing; should she fail to see that bonds of sentiment are essential to material interests; should her sons lose the energy, the heart, the ambition, whereby their fathers made her and her Empire what they are;

should she be smitten with the fear of Colonial responsibilities, and, following the faint-hearted advice of insular counsellors, regard these Isles as her Empire, and seek to contract its area to their limits, then, indeed, she will be *une puissance finie.* As yet, happily, Old England shows no symptoms of even incipient decay or decrepitude; but foreigners may sometimes be excused for mistaking the occasional timid, anti-colonial utterances and policy of some public speaker or writer as indicating the existence of such symptoms.

Our Imperial organization attracts the notice of foreigners. On September 13, 1879, appeared an article in the well-known French journal the *Moniteur,* which says:—"The bonds of Federation are the only ones suitable to the British Empire," and that it is "a certainty that the chief event marking the close of the century will be the general Federation of all the British possessions, bound firmly together in all its incoherent elements into an Empire of over two hundred and fifty million souls." The *Moniteur* adds:— "When subjected to a single impulse, the forces by sea and by land which the Empire could dispose of would be so colossal that they could only be counterbalanced by the Federation of other states, and the balance of power of Europe would have to be established on a new basis." Two years before the Franco-German war, M. Prevost Paradol, in his "La France Nouvelle," drew a brilliant picture of the future of the world, which he declared to be irrevocably Anglo-Saxon. Federation will soon make the American the leading branch of our race, unless we apply that system of union to the British Empire.

Napoleon said at St. Helena: "One of my great

ideas has been the agglomeration and concentration of the same nations, geographically considered, who have been scattered piecemeal by resolutions and policy. This agglomeration will take place sooner or later by the force of circumstances. This impulse is given, and I do not think that after my fall and the disappearance of my system, there will be any other great equilibrium possible than the agglomeration and confederation of great nations." In our days of steamers, railways, and telegraphs, Napoleon would never have thought that our Empire, "geographically considered," was not capable of such agglomeration; he would only have sighed that France had no such Colonial dominions as we possess for him to agglomerate with the old country.

We want some of the qualities of our French neighbours, as they have need of many of ours. If, with our practical capacity for working our institutions and modes of government, we had more of the inventiveness with which Frenchmen can frame political constitutions, we should have little difficulty in preparing beforehand a Federal organization, which could be applied the moment it was required. But instead of designing a symmetrical, constitutional structure before commencing to raise it up, our method is to construct piecemeal—a little now, an enlargement later on, an addition afterwards—until somehow or other we at length get what we want. Thus we may expect our Empire to become completely organized.

A great war—which may God avert!—would probably lead to its most speedy consolidation and organization; but should we not show our wisdom in being prepared beforehand for any great national emergency? The foe who would try to disintegrate

the Empire by force, would find he had adopted the
most certain means of welding it together. It has
been said that the Colonies may endeavour to escape
the consequences of some war, by deserting the Mother
Country when she is involved in it. No more atro-
cious slander was ever uttered. The whole past
history of the Colonies—the spirit with which they
have taken the side of England in past wars and
rumours of war, their recent offers to assist her
according to their means—all belie such a base
calumny. It is a gross insult, which in other words
declares them capable of acting the part of cowards
and poltroons. It is also a grave reflection upon the
honour of the Mother Country, to suppose she could
have produced offspring who could become so degenerate. No; "Blood is thicker than water!" as the
Colonies would prove in the hour of England's danger.

It will help us to see our way to the unity, and
organization of our Empire in the future, if we reflect
upon what must have happened, had a policy the
reverse of that pursued towards the United States
been adopted a century ago; had the wisdom of Lord
Rockingham and of Edmund Burke, instead of the
folly of George Grenville and of Lord North, pre-
vailed; had Colonial rights been respected, and Colonial
self-government existed as at present; had goodwill
and affection between England and the Colonies been
uninterrupted—what would have been the outcome
of it all? Americans of the third and fourth generation, the descendants of men who had been driven
from this country by political and religious persecu-
tion, were still warmly attached to old England, just
as all Colonists now are. They never thought of
separation till they were driven to it, and then it was

pain and grief to them to sever the old ties.[1] Had
they been in the happy position with respect to the
Mother Country of our present Colonies, what would
have happened? In another twenty years, England
became deeply involved in the wars with Napoleon;
and would the Americans have availed themselves of
the opportunity to sneak out of the Empire? They
would have scorned the idea, as all Colonists would
now do under similar circumstances. The great
French war would have united the American Colonies
more closely to England; for there is little doubt that
war-ships fitted out and manned by them would have
worthily responded to Nelson's immortal signal at
Trafalgar, and that regiments of them would have
shared the laurels of Wellington's army in the Penin-
sula and at Waterloo. Thus the Americans would
have established a claim to a voice in the Imperial
councils, and it would have been cheerfully granted
to them.

What then could have separated the United States
from the British Empire? Nothing![2] "Slavery,"

---

[1] "At length the Commonwealth was torn asunder. Two millions of Englishmen, who fifteen years before had been as loyal to
their prince and as proud of their country as the people of Kent
or Yorkshire, separated themselves by a solemn Act from the
Empire."—*Macaulay, Essay on the Earl of Chatham.*

[2] The *Times*, in a leading article of November 30, 1872, says
respecting Mr. Gladstone's observations on American Independence,
at the banquet to Mr. Cyrus Field: "If we disagree at all from
Mr. Gladstone's remarks on the original causes of separation, we
disagree from him in regarding that separation as inevitable.
When he says that Great Britain was struggling against nature,
and even against Providence, in opposing American Independence,
we take leave to doubt whether, if both nations had known their
own interests, American Independence would ever have been
proclaimed. Since it is now too late to undo, it is safe to regret
events which passed a century ago; and we hold ourselves
perfectly free to believe that, but for George III. and Lord North,
these Islands and the United Provinces might have continued

some one may perhaps say. But slavery was unable to sunder the South from the North; and could it have succeeded better against the North, backed by the whole British Empire? But even if the South had broken away, the best and most populous of the States would have remained with us.

Arguing from the past unhappy Colonial policy and experience of England, and from her present happy relations with her great Colonial dominions, we may well ask what is to prevent her union with them from being perpetual? Is it that some question with the strife-stirring bitterness of slavery can ever again arise? Is it because worse differences than those which at present exist, or have been amicably adjusted within recent years, are likely to disturb our harmony? Will a policy of Protection, which, though in some quarters carried to extremes, has failed to produce estrangement? Must oceans divide us nationally, in spite of the constant and rapid transit to and fro of so many of our people over them, between the most distant parts of our Empire, and in spite of the interchange of our ideas and feelings, electric sparks of sympathy, perpetually flying beneath them? Is it that, notwithstanding our vaunted intelligence, education, information, and the wonderful development of the Press in England and the Colonies, we are becoming more narrow and provincial in our sympathies, and parochial in our views, than our grandfathers, who, with less information, were more large-minded and national? Is it because the British

under the same Government—modified, no doubt, by the very nature of such association, yet still embodying the spirit of that Constitution which Burke's genius would have known how to develop." See also pages 17, 185.

race throughout the world is so bent on money-grubbing as to think so long as commerce can be carried on and flourish, "perish Empire, nationality, union"!—things which even our shrewd, practical American kinsmen so highly value? Have some wonderful economists and statisticians persuaded us, in spite of facts and figures, that the unity of the Empire is an unprofitable delusion, because, forsooth, they cannot make out a debtor and creditor account, showing in pounds, shillings, and pence its exact advantages? Is the legislative capacity, whereby we have adapted the institutions of the past to the circumstances of the present, going to fail us in providing for the requirements of the future? Are public men and statesmen, in all parts of the British dominions, going to become so engrossed in Provincial affairs, as not to be fired with the honourable ambition of seeking to take part in the legislation and administration of such a grand Empire as ours, if federated, must become?

What, then, do we want to effect the great object? Nothing but the will to carry it out, which so largely exists, and the organizing capacity of a nation endowed with all the grand institutions, rights, liberties, principles, and experiences essential to the maintenance and development of free and efficient government. In the early annals of the twentieth century, will have to be recorded the grandest success, or most lamentable failure, of a nation to utilize the most splendid materials the world ever furnished, for constructing the best and greatest of its Empires. May Heaven favour what promises such security, peace, freedom, and happiness upon earth!

Our whole subject is summed up in four sentences—

common defence involves common expense; common expense and danger confer the right of common control of foreign affairs, from which danger may arise, and of the forces required for defence; common control must be by common representation; common representation is Imperial Federation.

The words of the preamble of the writ of King Edward I.,[1] summoning the earliest regular English Parliament, in 1295, might well be used in summoning a Parliament of our present Empire: "It is a most equitable rule, that what concerns all should be approved by all; and common danger be repelled by united effort."

---

[1] Russell's "Modern Europe," vol. i. 390.

CHAPTER VII.

IMPERIAL DEFENCE.

(By Major Sir George S. Clarke, R.E., K.C.M.G.)

Absence of design in defence—Extent of possessions, population, and commerce to be defended—Modes of expansion of Britain and other Powers—Sea power and sea-borne trade—Interdependence of Imperial interests—Effects of war on English and Colonial trade—Interests of Empire must be defended as a whole—Importance of naval sufficiency and efficiency not realized—Doom awaiting naval inferiority—Royal commission on defence—Importance of Conference of 1887—Mr. Hofmeyr's proposal—Decision as to necessary strength of navy essential—Contribution to its maintenance—Definite permanent naval policy—Conferences to arrange contributions—Strength of military forces required—Fortified ports, defences, and troops in Australia, South Africa, and Canada—The West Indies—General principles of comprehensive scheme of defence—India—Standing Defence Committee with Colonial representatives—A Federation which is now possible.

An Empire built up by deliberate design, in pursuance of a defined and continuous policy, would escape the difficulties with which we are now confronted. Each fresh annexation would be made for an object previously considered; each new offshoot would start its political life under conditions laid down with an eye to the defensive strength of the whole. The general principles by which the fabric could be held together under the strain of war having been formulated and consistently upheld, the requirements of Imperial defence would be met as they arose, and power to resist aggression would steadily grow in proportion to the national development.

Of no Empire can this be exactly said; but expansion in accordance with principles deliberately fixed has received remarkable illustrations. The Romans unquestionably grasped the idea of Imperial defence, as it presented itself in their day, and long made it the basis of their policy. On the other hand, the Greeks failed in certainty of purpose, and their Colonies " tended to become rival states frequently at war with each other or with the Mother Country." Germany and Russia, in our own day, have expanded in obedience to deliberate design cherished and actively promoted by their respective dynasties. To both, territorial aggrandisement has consequently brought accession of strength. The founders of the United States devised a constitution under which a large territory has been gradually settled, successive additions bringing direct accession of wealth and power. But for the abnormal element introduced by the slave system, it is probable that smooth and unchecked development would have resulted.

In the creation of the British Empire, design has been conspicuously absent. The process has followed the general law of evolution. Here and there a great statesman may have marked and sought to guide the swift onward progress, or may have pondered as to how the inevitable requirements of the future were to be met. Great wars have forcibly directed attention to the strategic importance of particular points, and have left their impress upon the national policy; but the lessons were not all applied, and the readjustments, which followed upon long contests in which Great

Britain played a leading part, do not always show either clear purpose or adequate foresight. The incentive to expansion appears to have been supplied and maintained mainly by commercial rivalry, impelling forward a race which cherishes a strong aversion to militarism. It is natural that questions of Imperial defence should have been neglected. Wherever profitable trade was capable of being established, wherever a new territory appeared suited to the colonizing proclivities of the Anglo-Saxon, there must the flag be planted. How it was to be maintained, how the new acquisition would act and react upon the national strength, were matters easily overlooked. ⁄

To this strong impulse of commercial rivalry, Professor Seeley has ably traced the real origin of a long series of great wars, which shattered the older systems of Portugal, Spain, Holland, and France, and left Great Britain prominent as a Colonial power. Since 1815, the process of extension has steadily advanced. The one European war in which we have been involved was inspired by fears for the security of our communications with the East, and of the numerous minor struggles, extending down to the recent Matabele conflict, expansion for commercial purposes has been either the direct motive or the indirect occasion.

Thus has grown up an Empire spread over the whole world, capricious in its distribution, largely heterogeneous in its elements, diverse in its political and economic conditions. An island Continent ruled by five mutually independent administrations; a vast Asiatic territory, won and held by military force, and now marching with Russia, China, and perhaps France; a great portion of North America, with three thousand miles of frontier shared by a nation of

seventy millions of English-speaking people ; a group
of progressive Colonies in South Africa, with spheres
and protectorates scarcely explored ; isolated stations
in all lands, from Gibraltar carved out of Spain, to
Kowloon marked off from China ; islands in every sea,
from the great fortress of Malta to Fanning in the
centre of the Pacific—such are the territorial elements
of Greater Britain.   Of forms of government there is
an ascending chain from remote Tristan d'Acunha,
which appears to take care of itself, through Crown
systems varying in type, to Canada with virtual independence.   A population of more than 360 millions
dwells under the flag, which also covers an annual
sea-borne trade of about 970 millions sterling.

Such an Empire finds no parallel in history.   " The
Romans," writes Sir A. Lyall,[1] "once united under an
extensive dominion a number of subject provinces,
client kingdoms, protected allies, races and tribes, by
a system of conquest. . . . But the Roman dominions
were compact and well knit together by solid communications."   The modern Empire of Germany is
compact in territory as in race and climatic conditions.
Russia is swiftly building up a great Asiatic dominion,
but is proceeding with deliberate purpose and a clear
view to defensive requirements.   " With the Roman,
Russian, and all other historical Empires, the mass of
their territory has been acquired by advancing step by
step from the central starting-point, making one foot-
hold sure before another was taken, firmly placing one
arch of the viaduct before another was thrown out,
allowing no interruption of territorial coherence from
the centre to the circumference."   With us the process
has differed absolutely, and security for the future has

[1] " The Rise of the British Dominion in India."

not been the main or even a principal object sought after. Our expansion has followed more nearly the methods of Portugal, Holland, and Spain, which led to disruption and disaster. The Colonial systems of the two former Powers fell from inability to maintain inviolate their home territory; that of the latter was destroyed by reason of incapacity to secure its sea communications. Here are two historical lessons of vital import.

The expansion of Great Britain, unlike that of Rome, of Russia, and of the United States, has taken place *by the sea alone.* Although, as Captain Mahan has clearly shown, the Romans, in their great contest with Carthage, owed everything to the command of the Mediterranean, their territorial extension was not, as ours has been, limited solely to regions approached by sea, nor were the communications between the Mother Country and the outlying members maritime alone. Shorn of her transmarine possessions, Rome might still have remained a great power, as is Germany to-day, although the consolidation of purely military strength throughout a large area, however compact, was far more difficult in her day than in our own.

For us, however, existence depends upon sea power alone. The conditions which would render possible the foreign conquest of one member, would threaten all alike. General dismemberment would inevitably follow such naval defeat as France expefienced at the beginning of this century. To an Empire whose entire fabric is supported by sea-borne commerce, the loss of maritime communications means ruin.

All over the world is spread the gigantic and intensely complex network of British trade, creating a

K

mutual interdependence of interests between the members of the Empire, such as has never before existed. The prosperity of each depends on this trade. A mere temporary depression entails distress; cessation would mean widespread disaster. From the little Colony of Turks Island, with its total exports and imports of £62,000,[1] to the great Australasian group with nearly £132,000,000, each member is deriving its existence from sea-borne trade. None can suffer without entailing corresponding loss elsewhere. Every fluctuation in the United Kingdom is felt throughout the Empire, every loss to any Colony reacts instantly upon the Mother Country. This extreme sensitiveness of the system to the minor disturbances which occur in peace supplies a gauge of what the interruption of communications in war must involve. In his memorable words at the Conference of 1887, Mr. Deakin employed no mere figure of speech.

"We cannot imagine any description of circumstances by which the Colonies should be humiliated or their powers lessened, under which the Empire would not be itself humiliated, weakened, and lessened. And we are unable to conceive any conditions under which the wealth and status of the Colonies could be increased, which would not increase in the same measure the wealth and status of the Empire."

These words fitly embody a great truth, which has not even now received the full recognition accorded to it by the brilliant Chief Secretary of Victoria. The "Little England party," if it ever existed as a political force, has been happily submerged; but indications are not wanting, at home and in the Colonies, of false conceptions of the primary conditions of our national existence. "Trade," it is said, "is cosmopolitan. It

[1] Figures for 1889.

cares for no flag, knows no patriotism, and is independent of national sentiment. Were our Colonies to break adrift, or pass into other hands, we could still trade with them without loss of mutual profit." From the other side, it has been publicly asserted that connection with the Empire involves undue risks, and may lead to participation in wars with which Colonies have no concern; that declarations of independence would follow an outbreak of hostilities between the Mother Country and a foreign Power; and that trade would either be permitted to pass free under some newly-invented flag, or would easily transfer itself to the flag of some unspecified neutral.

Such assertions are radically and dangerously false.

It is true that of the total trade of the Mother Country a large proportion goes to foreign countries, and in this it may be contended that Greater Britain has no direct interest. In the case of the Colonies, on the other hand, by far the greater portion of their commerce is with the United Kingdom; and even if it were possible in war to separate the two, and secure entire immunity from Colonial property afloat, it is evident that any loss affecting the Mother Country would instantly cripple her power of trading with her scattered members, and would react upon them with fatal effect. No line, however, could or would be drawn by an enemy. The greater part of the Colonial products sent to the United Kingdom might be claimed as good prize of war. Thus not only would the commerce on which the Colonies live be imperilled, whether they asserted their independence or not, but the mere weakening of the all-important home market would, apart from the direct loss, involve widespread ruin.

The following figures show the distribution of Colonial commerce in 1889.

GROUP.	IMPORTS FROM			EXPORTS TO		
	United Kingdom. £	British Colonies. £	Elsewhere. £	United Kingdom. £	British Colonies. £	Elsewhere. £
Australasia	30,030,413	31,842,108	7,165,961	29,269,187	28,594,999	5,085,951
Africa	11,970,110	1,630,230	2,186,866	11,595,412	2,083,106	1,459,993
North America ...	10,653,130	1,235,761	15,888,839	9,827,373	1,119,450	11,820,642
Asia (excluding India, etc.)	7,219,827	14,988,054	9,364,054	7,146,370	8,897,561	10,552,427
West Indies	2,648,017	777,961	2,585,702	2,086,885	509,327	4,714,260

The preponderance of Colonial trade within the Empire over that with foreign countries is thus enormous in the case of the Australasian, African, and Asian groups. In the West Indies, the preponderance is small, and in North America, on account of the proximity of the United States markets, external trade predominates.

The figures strikingly illustrate the mutual interdependence of the members of the Empire and the sterling truth of Mr. Deakin's words. No member could abandon its allegiance in war without courting financial disaster. Its external trade would not suffice for the needs of its population. Its vital resources must remain bound up with the fortunes of the nation as a whole. No other flag could possibly cover them in war, even if the great legal difficulties of a wholesale transfer of shipping, officers, and crews to another nationality could be overcome.

Conversely, the loss of a trade with her Colonies, amounting to £124,624,464, in 1889 (India and Burmah excluded), would bring untold suffering upon the Mother Country. As Sir John Robinson well said,[1] " If Greater Britain should fall to pieces, then God help Great Britain."

Facts are inexorable. The markets of the United Kingdom are essential to the well-being of the Colonies, and could not be replaced; the Colonial markets are vital to the United Kingdom. It is of course conceivable that these conditions might change in the future, and that the home markets might cease in certain cases to be of value to a particular Colony—Turks Island and the Virgin Islands, for example, at present export little or nothing to the Mother Country—but

[1] Conference of 1887.

with the larger Colonies any great diversion of trade is most improbable. And even of the small trade of Turks Island, nearly one fourth goes to markets within the Empire, and might be destroyed if those markets passed into other hands.

Reared on a commercial basis, knit together by innumerable and ever-increasing commercial ties, the splendid fabric of the Empire must be defended as a whole. Heterogeneous as are, in a sense, its many members, they are united by one supreme common interest—the protection of the sea communications between each other and the Mother Country.

For us, therefore, Imperial defence rests entirely upon maritime strength. If the navy proves unable to maintain the sea communications of the Empire in war, all other preparations will be of no avail. If this condition is unfulfilled, no other forces can be brought into play. On the sufficiency and efficiency of the navy the national safety absolutely depends. This has been so often said as to be now almost a platitude; but full recognition of all that is implied has not yet been accorded, and in Greater Britain especially the paramount necessity of retaining the command of the sea has not been adequately grasped.

In a remarkable article, written twenty-four years ago,[1] Mr. Gladstone forcibly drew attention to this defective sense of imagination.

"It is hard to say whether or when our countrymen will be fully alive to the vast advantages they derive from consummate means of naval defence. . . . Our lot would perhaps be too much favoured, if we possessed, together with such advantages, a full sense of what they are. Where the Almighty grants

[1] *Edinburgh Review*, October, 1870.

exceptional and peculiar benefits, He sometimes permits, by way of counterpoise, an insensibility to their value."

As has been already pointed out, the explanation of this mental obscuration is to be sought in the very processes by which the Empire was created. Trade, having supplied the initial impulse, became an absorbing interest. Each new settlement, engaged from the first in vigorously combating difficulties of all kinds, could not give a thought to Imperial defence. The early struggles being ended, the thriving community grew into a great self-governing Colony, intensely preoccupied with the solution of its own many problems. It might, and frequently did, regard questions of local defence, but could not be expected to take up an Imperial standpoint.

Meanwhile, the Mother Country, half-bewildered by the rapidity of an expansion which she had not designed and could not restrain, more and more engrossed in island politics, and weighted with the grave responsibilities of India, gave little heed to the higher policy of defence. Even now the working classes appear to be under the delusion that mere local legislation can meet all their needs. There is no one to teach them that their prosperity depends entirely upon security of commerce of which the navy is the only possible guarantee. So far, the Board School system has failed in one of its first duties—that of inculcating the idea of the mutual interdependence of Great and Greater Britain. The very geographical conditions of the Empire have contributed to the clouding of the national imagination. Communications, visible and palpable, such as roads, railways, and rivers, appeal directly to the mind. The necessity for their maintenance is being continually enforced;

their risks are understood and provided against. The pathless seas, however, create no such impression. Ships come and go, and the growing ease, speed, and certainty of maritime transit lures us, who have not known naval war, into forgetfulness of the doom which awaits naval inferiority. Wide-reaching, all-embracing, are the operations of maritime commerce; as wide-reaching is the disaster to which it is liable.

Thus, till recent years, the problem of Imperial defence has received little attention. A long period of somnolence was at length broken by the Crimean War, which threw a vivid light upon the forgotten needs of the army, but did not raise larger questions. In 1859, an ebullition of coast fortifications across the Channel produced—by some confusion of ideas—a costly rejoinder in kind along the shores of England. At about the same time, the rehabilitation of the four fortresses abroad was commenced on traditional principles, rather than with an eye to the national problem. After heavy expenditure, thus applied, the war scare of 1878 found the Empire as a whole quite unprepared, and alarm out of all proportion to the then risks was the natural result. While the local defence of the British islands had occupied many minds, that of the trade by which those islands exist had been generally ignored.

The Royal Commission, presided over by the late Earl of Carnarvon, was the first official recognition of the defensive needs of Greater Britain. Nevertheless, the terms of the reference excluded the ruling factor —the strength of the navy—and the recommendations were, in the main, demands for fortification. Valuable figures were, however, brought together, indicating clearly that the great stake of the nation was trade at sea. Coaling stations were selected with reference to the trade routes, and many admirable suggestions were thrown out. The proceedings were necessarily lengthy, and the full reports were not completed till 1882, to remain as secret documents for five years. In the meantime, coast batteries of little value were hastily erected at certain stations abroad, and in some Colonies vigorous independent action was inaugurated.

The scare of 1885 found the fortifications recommended by the Royal Commission incomplete and partially unarmed, though great progress had been made in the works undertaken in Australia. In numerous Colonies, fears were loudly expressed, and arms were freely applied for. The general desire for fixed defences was marked; the fact that the danger lay at sea rather than on shore was rarely recognized. Out of this second scare arose the Colonial Defence Committee, by which it was sought to supply the reasoned advice evidently needed, and to provide the machinery for the discussion of questions of Imperial defence.

A further and most important step was taken in convening the Conference of 1887. Here, for the first time, the statesmen of Greater Britain were brought into direct contact with each other, and with the heads of the home administration. The questions discussed included important matters relating to defence. The occasion was memorable, and the debates were eminently worthy of the occasion. On all sides the keen desire to weld together the scattered members of the Empire and enable them to undertake common preparations for defence was conspicuous; but, as was natural, the conditions of the problem appeared to have been misunderstood in some quarters. Opinion in the great Colonies had formed itself almost without help or guidance, and the fascinations of fixed defences had in some cases obscured real issues.

The Conference was a signal success. The outstanding question of an Australasian subvention to naval votes, in return for an increase in the squadron, was settled, and a great principle of national policy thereby recognized. Mr. Hofmeyr, in a remarkable paper, advocated an Imperial customs tariff providing a differential duty of 2 per cent. throughout the Empire on all imports from foreign countries, the proceeds, estimated at seven millions sterling per annum, to be set aside for Imperial defence. This striking proposal was made with a view to compel attention to the principle of a common liability in regard to really national needs, rather than as a formal subject of debate. Speaking for the Dutch population of South Africa, Mr. Hofmeyr stated—

"They hold that, so long as no system of federation or of government in which they are represented has been hit upon or developed, so long they cannot be expected to be in duty bound to defend themselves against the European enemies of England. But, at the same time, they acknowledge that there are very great advantages, and, belonging to the British Empire, they share whether they will or not; and therefore they are ready and prepared to do something."

Traces of the same sentiment appeared in the minds of other speakers, indicating clearly the difficulty of administering any national fund without having resort to representation in some form.

The Conference was quickly followed by a naval scare, well grounded and actively promoted by the great commercial bodies of the United Kingdom, and by the home press; but not supported, as it should have been, by the unanimous voice of the Empire, although Mr. Hofmeyr had clearly stated his belief that the strength of the navy was inadequate. The ship-building authorized by the Naval Defence Act, which was forced upon the Administration, is now nearly completed, and already we are face to face with a new scare, suddenly raised, and having its origin in a few descriptive letters setting forth the strength of the French squadron in the Mediterranean and the resources of Toulon—matters easily ascertainable by any one who desired to master the present naval situation.

While progress has thus been made since 1887, it is clear that, though the conditions of the problem are better understood than formerly, no solution has been attained. Lord Salisbury's words to the Conference: "We are all sensible that this meeting is the beginning of a state of things which is to have great results in the future," remain to be fulfilled, and the initiative can come from the Imperial Government alone. Great and Greater Britain have fortified their ports at vast cost; they dispose of a full million of armed men; they have not as yet finally decided what is the necessary strength of the one arm on which all depends. Upon this decision hang the whole defensive preparations of the Empire, the scale of all its fortifications, and the strength of the greater portion of its military forces. The problem has hitherto been approached at the wrong end. If the navy fails to guard the sea-communications, the Empire will crumble under the first strain; the loss of India is inevitable; the conversion of every harbour into an impregnable fortress will avail nothing. The *movement* of trade is the life, breath of the nation. If it is stifled, the whole body will perish.

The navy is, therefore, the force in which every member of the Empire is directly interested—the force by which alone they are linked together. Given the condition of full naval superiority, such as has existed at various periods of our history, then maritime communications become superior to all others. Failing the fulfilment of this condition, they are of all the most easily and disastrously assailable.

But the requisite supremacy is as easily attainable now as in 1759, of which period Voltaire wrote, "The English had never such a superiority at sea as at this time." And, after pointing to successive defeats of the navies of Henry IV., Louis XIII., and Louis XIV., he proceeded to ask, "What can be the reason of this continued superiority? Is it not that the sea, which the French can live well enough without, is essentially necessary to the English, and that nations always succeed best in those things for which they have an absolute occasion."

There is only one way to bring home the first axiom of Imperial defence to the national mind at home and abroad. Each member must contribute to the naval strength of the whole. The difficulty of inaugurating this arrangement is capable of easy exaggeration. At the present moment the Colonies of Australasia, of their free will, contribute £120,000 per annum to naval votes. It is true that this subsidy is coupled with conditions; but the conditions were patriotically defined by the Colonies concerned, and will not fetter the free action of the squadron in war. Other Colonies contribute considerable sums in aid of army funds. These could at once be diverted, and the change would be popular. It is hopeless to aim at any rational basis for the apportionment of military burdens between the United Kingdom and such Colonies as Singapore or Hong Kong; but these Colonies depend absolutely upon sea-borne trade, and would acquiesce in sharing the cost of the only force which can protect it. A Colonial naval contribution could be equitably calculated upon the imports and exports, and would follow their rise or fall. If, from the whole Empire, a mere £250,000—more than this is already paid to Imperial funds—were forthcoming in the first instance, at least a great principle would be established. The claim to protest against the inadequacy of the navy would arise, and its influence would be felt.[1] To every member the sense of participation in one supreme interest would be forcibly brought home. As Mr. Hofmeyr said of his proposal, but in a higher degree, it "would establish a connecting-link between the Colonies mutually as well as between the Colonies and the Empire, such as is not at present in existence, and which might develop by-and-by into a most powerful bond of union."

A new building programme will shortly be announced, which may for the time allay the public alarm. Until, however, a full inquiry has been made into the duties of the navy in war, and the best means of enabling it to fulfil those duties, no stability of opinion will be attained, and recurring scares are inevitable. A navy has many other requirements than ships, and the maintenance of a just balance between these requirements means efficiency. It is not another building programme which is needed, but the laying down of a definite naval policy upon per-

---

[1] Already this claim has been advanced by the Australasian Colonies, and with success, as regards the superabundant squadron maintained in their waters.

manent lines. Such a body as the Commission of 1879 could indicate such a policy, and consequently provide a solid foundation for Imperial defence; but it is necessary that Greater Britain should be represented in its councils.

No naval contribution, however small, should be sought without summoning a new Conference, and clearly explaining the scope and objects of the new departure. Crown Colonies naturally resent a ukase, and, like self-governing communities, claim to be reasoned with. When it is remembered that four Crown Colonies freely voted handsome sums in aid of fixed defences, there need be little fear of securing agreement. The contribution having been settled, would remain an unchanged percentage of the value of the imports and exports, unless modified at future Conferences held at intervals of five years. At these periodical Conferences, questions requiring joint action between the members of the Empire would be freely discussed, and at the same time the Colonies would have the opportunity of making direct representations in regard to naval matters, and, as in 1887, of receiving direct information from the Admiralty officials. From this small beginning, however rudimentary, important results would spring; for a great principle would receive practical recognition.

The policy of maintaining a national navy able to guard the communications of the Empire in war with any reasonably probable combination of Powers, having been definitely adopted as the basis of Imperial defence, and the means to permanently guarantee this main object having been taken, the functions of the remaining elements can be rationally adjusted. The safety of the heart of the Empire will be secured, as in the past, upon the seas; but while invasion will be wholly impossible, and the maintenance of large bodies of men merely for home defence unnecessary, descents upon the coast line have to be provided against, and power to rapidly concentrate an efficient force of all arms must be retained.

The strength of the regular forces will, however, be determined by the demands of India and certain Colonial garrisons. Merely to fulfil these demands in peace-time, a considerable standing army is required; but the organization must be such as to enable a reinforcement of at least 60,000 men to be sent to India at short notice, and to provide about 10,000 men for a small war or for expeditionary forces in a great war. The primary requirement of our military system at home is, therefore, to maintain and rapidly reinforce troops abroad. Whether this requirement can best be fulfilled by the modified European organization now existing cannot be here discussed.

The armaments and standing garrisons of the fortified ports of the Empire would be determined by the condition that raids only could be attempted against them, such raids, however, varying in force with geographical position. The cost in the case of the fortresses and the coaling stations selected by the Royal Commission should be borne by the Home Exchequer, all Colonial contributions being devoted to naval funds.

Under existing arrangements, the self-governing Colonies of Australasia undertake the responsibility of their local defence; but the nature of that responsibility has not been fully understood, and the patriotism of these Colonies has led them to large expenditure upon objects which have not been always well chosen.

As has been pointed out, "Attack on the Australasian littoral reduces itself to raids by an enemy's cruisers based on his defended ports," and moderate fixed defences, well organized, will suffice for the needs of harbours so remote from the naval centres of other Powers. Much more than this may, however, be counted upon from the strong public spirit of these great Colonies. The rôle of their troops "is not likely to be limited to the passive defence of ports little liable to attack." They have already done good service in the Soudan, and if the Empire were involved in war, Australasia would seek and obtain, not merely security, but solid guarantees for the future. While the aid of Australian troops, if freely offered, should be accepted for service in any part of the Empire, a zone should be defined which should be considered as being within their sphere of action. This involves organization on a uniform basis, assimilation of terms of service, and certain special measures of preparation, which could only be taken by the central military authority of the group. Already the defence of Thursday Island and King George's Sound has been provided for on a federal basis, and there is no reason why federation for military purposes should be delayed.

In South Africa, the definition of responsibility is far less clear. The home Government has not only provided entirely for the defence of the small naval station at Simons Bay, but has supplied an armament for the all-important mercantile port of Table Bay, and maintains a regular garrison. The future development of the harbours of Port Elizabeth and East London may justify small measures of local defence, which should be undertaken by the Colony, as those of Durban have been provided entirely by Natal.

The Colonial forces in South Africa are considerable and contain excellent material, but their organization is capable of improvement. Assuming no serious native troubles, an ample force would be available for local defence and also to provide contingents for operations which might have a direct bearing on South African interests. The development of this important position of the Empire is rapidly proceeding, and the future will probably see a strong federation to which, as to Australia, a sphere of action could fitly be assigned. Meanwhile, to the Cape Colony, with a total sea-borne trade of about nine millions entering and leaving a single port, the supreme interest lies, as Mr. Hofmeyr has recognized, in naval ascendancy.

Canada possesses no defended ports except Esquimalt, to be provided with an armament by the Mother Country, which also maintains a much fortified naval station at Halifax. On the other hand, Canada maintains a small permanent force and a militia about 30,000 strong, with a large nominal reserve of men who have passed through its ranks. In organization and equipment this militia force is at present defective; but much of the personnel is of admirable quality, and, under proper arrangements, Canada could, in war, relieve the infantry garrison of Halifax and provide a strong contingent for any Imperial service. This, rather than defence of the long land frontier, should be her recognized rôle; for the time is approaching when closer relations with the United States will be established, with mutual benefit to the two great English-speaking nations.

As to the distinctive group formed by the West

L

Indian Islands, a clear policy has been publicly announced, "based upon the broad principle that the protection of the West Indies, as a whole, must depend upon the navy acting in sufficient force, and that the Imperial defences on shore should be such only as will facilitate the operations of the navy in keeping the sea clear of hostile vessels." Two naval stations, selected by the Royal Commission, have been fortified and will be maintained at the charge of the United Kingdom. In the case of other islands, local defence is left to individual effort; but, in some instances, assistance has been given in the form of arms, and this policy should be more liberally pursued in regard to any Colony which evinces military spirit. The protection of private property against a raid by a single cruiser can thus be obtained at small cost, and every port denied to an enemy's vessels in these waters is something gained to the national cause.

The general principles on which it is sought to base a comprehensive scheme of Imperial defence may now be briefly summarized.

The navy to be maintained at a strength amply sufficient to secure the communications of the Empire in war, to be supported by every member in some proportion to its stake upon the seas, to be regarded as distinctively national, but to be centrally administered, by which alone complete and uniform efficiency can be secured. This will not exclude decentralization of stores, rendering each naval station as independent as possible, nor the creation of a naval reserve in connection with each station.

Conferences, at which the Colonies would be represented, to be held at regular periods, in order that the general situation may be reviewed, Imperial questions settled, and the bonds of union drawn closer by the recognition of common needs.

Local defence to be decentralized as far as possible, but responsibility to be extended by grouping. Such decentralization, however, to be controlled in the sense that the necessary standard of defence is made to conform to the general requirements of the group, which would entail special consideration in each case.

The responsibility for the defence of India to remain with the United Kingdom, whose standing army would be organized with this view and having regard to the other duties above specified. In certain cases, however, Colonial garrisons would be available in war, setting free regular troops for the purpose of expeditions. Given an adequate navy, the natural rôle of the army becomes offensive.

In order to secure a constant watch over the requirements of the Empire as a whole, and to discuss and settle the numerous questions directly or indirectly connected with Imperial defence, a standing committee to which Colonial representatives have free access is essential. The Colonial Defence Committee as now constituted would meet these requirements; but every Agent-General should be an *ex-officio* member, and every Colony should be able to appoint a representative to take personal charge of any question and to share in its discussion.

While evidently the establishment of federation by groups would facilitate the application of the above principles, nothing has been advocated which involves any organic change.

The existing resources of the Empire are sufficient for every need; its manhood possesses unrivalled

vigour. All that is needed is the direction of effort
on a uniform plan by which the enormous potential
strength of the Empire could be quickly and smoothly
brought to the aid of its defence. Federation, in the
sense of well-ordered preparation for a national emergency, is *now* possible; and such federation, once accomplished, would bring about results far-reaching.

The sense of general insecurity produced by panics
constantly recurring, is an agent of disintegration.
Weakness is incompatible with proper national pride.
Strength, visible and unquestioned, can alone guarantee
enduring union. Of such strength, the navy is the
very essence.

CHAPTER VIII.

THE CONTRACTION OF ENGLAND AND ITS ADVOCATES.

Professor Seeley's *Expansion of England*—Articles with same title
by Mr. John Morley and Mr. Goldwin Smith—M. Prévost-
Paradol on "the ascendancy of the Anglo-Saxon race"—
The philosophy of contraction and disruption—Mr. Frederic
Harrison and "the reduction of the Empire"—Mr. Morley's
objection on fiscal grounds; his attempt to answer Mr.
Forster; opposed to views of Sir Alex. Galt, Sir Henry
Parkes, and Mr. Service—Position in Federation of smaller
possessions—What could be offered Colonies in return for
help?—Would they assist in wars not concerning them?—
Mandat impératif against such wars—Difficulties about
"Federal Council"—"Mother of Parliaments" would sink
to be a State legislature—Difficulties in forming Intercolonial Federation—Mr. Wm. Forster of New South Wales
on "The Fallacies of Federation"—Separation by oceans—
Gains and sacrifices by England and the Colonies—"An
artificial Centralization"—A great modern Roman Empire—
England overtaxing her strength—Englishmen distrusting
their Country—Lamentations of Mr. Goldwin Smith—The
"motley heritage"—India—Challenge to Federalists to produce plan—"British ignorance of the Colonies"—"England
would have to defend Colonies"—They would not "maintain
army or navy"—"Want of National spirit in the Colonies"—
Harm done by Lord Dufferin—Galvanizing the dead cause
of disintegration—Shrivelling prescriptions of insular philosophy.

It is not to be expected that any great policy can be
proposed without encountering the opposition of men,
viewing it from different standpoints and influenced
by various motives; and the more the policy commends
itself to approval, the smarter often becomes the fire
from the great guns of criticism, especially when left

isolated and unsupported. In the following article, published in the *National Review* of June, 1884, I attempted to deal with the chief objections of the ablest opponents of Imperial Federation—

Seldom is such a striking contribution made to our collection of household words as that presented by Professor Seeley, in the name of his attractive work, " The Expansion of England." This title, which is so in harmony with the arguments and conclusions of the author, has also been appropriated by two other writers,[1] to head articles which are remarkable for being entirely out of accord with it. Had the titles of these contributions of Mr. John Morley and Mr. Goldwin Smith been consistent with their contents, they would have been—" The Contraction of England," " The Curtailment of Great Britain," " The Disruption of the Empire "—or something equally repellent to all true Britons; but it was too much, even for the philosophy of the writers, to place at the heads of their articles the bare statement of their exact design.

Mr. Seeley contends that " expansion is the chief character of English history in the eighteenth century," and that " the explanation of that Second Hundred Years' War between England and France, which fills the eighteenth century, is this, that they were rival candidates for the possession of the New World." The actors in the great drama of the eighteenth century may not have even dreamed of what they were bringing about; but to the men of the nineteenth century the most patent, tangible result achieved by our grandfathers, has been the expansion of England

[1] Mr. John Morley, in *Macmillan's Magazine* for February, 1884, and Professor Goldwin Smith, in the *Contemporary Review* for April, 1884.

in the West, and in the East, and in the South.
Multitudes of men who know little, and care less,
about the Spanish Succession, the Austrian Succession,
and the Seven Years' War, are fully sensible of the
great fact that the race, religion, and language of
England are firmly established over the vast regions
of North America and Australasia, and that we possess
a great Indian Empire. It well fits in with the
belief of those who hold that an over-ruling Providence
controls the affairs of men and of nations, that what,
at the time of the occurrence of the great wars of
last century, might have been regarded as a mere
secondary object, should have turned out to be of
transcendent importance.

The great contest for New World expansion is clearly
appreciated by Mr. Seeley, as also by that brilliant
French writer of the Second Empire, M. Prevost-
Paradol, who in his "La France Nouvelle," published
two years before the Franco-German War, vividly
depicts the great result of the struggles of last century
—"the ascendancy of the Anglo-Saxon race outside
Europe." He says, speaking as a Frenchman, "We
might in former times have asked if our race and
language should not prevail over all others, and if it
were not the French form which European civilization
would assume to overrun the rest of the world? All
the chances," he continues, "were on our side. It
was France who, through Canada and Louisiana, began
to overspread North America; India seemed given up
to us"; and further on he remarks, "that since
extended navigation has opened up the entire globe
to the enterprise of European races, three people have,
as it were, been tried, each in its turn, by destiny, in
order to be invested with the leadership in the future

of the human race, in propagating everywhere their language and their blood, by means of durable colonies, and by moulding, as it were, the world to their image. One would have believed in the sixteenth century that Spanish civilization would have spread itself over all the earth; but some irremediable vices speedily shattered that Colonial power, the *débris* of which, still covering a vast area, testifies to its ephemeral grandeur; we have been tried in our turn, as Louisiana and Canada bear melancholy witness. At last came England, by whom the great work is definitively accomplished."

Whether Mr. Seeley is right or wrong in his historical deductions, his conclusions as to the future stand unaffected by literary criticism, as to his "fancy weaving a web of connection over any group of historical facts." He has no doubt given critics, whose business is to differ from the originators of ideas—for to agree would be to relinquish their functions and acknowledge a leader—scope for literary comment. This, however, will not avail to draw intelligent readers of "The Expansion of England" from the clear and certain conclusion which it is intended to emphasize, namely, that "if the United States and Russia hold together for another half century, they will at the end of that time completely dwarf such old European states as France and Germany, and depress them into the second class. They will do the same for England if . . . she still thinks of herself as simply a European state." There is, of course, the alternative that the United States and Russia may not hold together. Perhaps schools of Infallible-oracular-doctrinaires may arise among the people of those nations, to convert them to the philosophy of con-

traction and disruption;[1] or, as prophets are not without honour save in their own country, Professor Goldwin Smith, Mr. John Morley, and also Mr. Frederic
Harrison—who has recently declared that one of the
"three great ends in politics which he has specially
at heart" is "to prepare for the inevitable reduction
of the Empire"—could perhaps be spared to go as
missionaries of the new creed of national disintegration, to Americans and Russians, who might possibly
be more easily convinced of its wisdom than Englishmen
seem inclined to be. We sometimes hear suggestions
of general disarmament. Perhaps our wise men of the
future may not only be able to carry this out, but
also to bring about a general contraction of expanded
nations, so that, with her Colonies cast adrift, England
should not be dwarfed.

When Mr. John Morley ceases to deal with impracticable modes of federation, which Federalists above
all other men should be glad to see exploded, he ceases
to do harm to the cause of Federal Union. Take,
for example, one of his objections, which has previously
been urged by weaker opponents. He assumes that a
uniform fiscal policy in all the dominions of a Federated
Empire would be indispensable but unattainable, and
quotes, as conclusive against federation, the words of
Sir Thomas Farrer: "Free Trade is of extreme importance, but Freedom is more important still." A
Federalist can easily endorse this; for whatever may
be his views on political economy, he—though re-
gretting that there may be but little hope of their

---

[1] Carlyle speaks of "Serenely beautiful philosophizing, with its
soft moonshiny clearness and thinness;" and now, reader, "behold
you have it!"—to again quote the author of so many telling
expressions.

universal acceptance throughout the Empire—would
not be so narrow as to seek to enforce them by a
Federal Constitution; seeing that a uniform fiscal
system would be no more essential to the union of the
Empire under a Federal Government, than it is at
the present time to the union of England with the
Dominion of Canada and the Colony of Victoria, which,
in spite of their protective tariffs, are both among the
best customers of the manufacturers of this country.

Mr. Forster, a practical statesman, with large
sympathies, makes, in his famous Edinburgh address,
some very simple, common-sense remarks, to the effect
that if the people of the Empire are imbued "with the
desire that the union should last," this "idea will
realize itself," and that, "when the time comes, it
will be found that where there's a will there's a way"
of organizing the union. To this, Mr. Morley has
nothing but mere assertion to offer in reply—which,
if weighed against mere assertion on Mr. Forster's
side, would not move the scale,—for this is the
attempted answer: "The will depends upon the way;
and the more any possible way of federation is considered the less likely is there to be the will." This
is asserted in face of the fact that the more federation
is discussed, the more its adherents increase, both in
England and the Colonies. The ex-Premier of New
South Wales, Sir Henry Parkes, has spoken in sympathy with organized union, and the present Premier
of Victoria, Mr. Service, has recently emphatically
declared for Federation, expressing the hope that he
may yet sit in an Imperial Federal Legislature. Sir
Alexander Galt, and other leading Canadians, have
also for some time been its advocates. Indeed, Mr.
Morley himself, at the beginning of his article—in a

passage which is rather inconsistent with that just quoted—says: " Mr. Seeley's book . . . has helped, and will still further help, to swell a sentiment that was already slowly rising to full flood."

Mr. Morley wonders what place in the federation " would be given to possessions of the class of the West Indies, Mauritius, the West Coast . . . Gibraltar, Malta, Aden, and Hong Kong." Mr. Goldwin Smith is also troubled with a similar difficulty. It surely cannot be seriously contended that, even if insuperable obstacles were to prevent these places from being represented, or that, with the exception of the West Indies, they were all too inconsiderable to have even one member in the Parliament of the Empire, the idea of the federation of Canada, Australasia, and South Africa, with the Mother Country must be abandoned.

Mr. Morley also inquires " what have we to offer to Australia in return for joining us in a share of such obligations," as the possessions just referred to entail? and he remarks that " it would hardly be either an advantage or a pleasure to the people of a young country, with all their busy tasks hot on their hands, to be interrupted by the duty of helping by men or cash to put down an Indian Mutiny." Nearly thirty years ago, when Australia was in a state of actual infancy, she was about to raise a regiment to send to India, when the mutiny was suppressed. Recently, also, some of her local forces were offered for service in South Africa, when the war suddenly came to an end. She also contributed largely to the Patriotic Fund at the time of the Crimean War, and to the Indian Mutiny and Famine Relief Funds. Had Mr. Morley known these facts, he surely would not have written as he has done; and it is very unfortunate for his argument that, just as his article appeared, the Government of Victoria was offering to place the gunboats of the Colony at the disposal of the Imperial authorities for service in the Red Sea. Canada has not been behind Australia in willingness to help the Mother Country, having offered material aid when war with Russia was anticipated a few years ago; and considering that she possesses the third largest mercantile marine in the world, she would bring much strength to the United Empire, which would principally require naval defence.

If Colonies would render assistance in India and other Oriental wars, *à fortiori*, they would do so when the interests of other Colonies were concerned. Mr. Morley asks: " Is it possible to suppose that the Canadian lumberman and the Australian sheep-farmer will cheerfully become contributors to a Greater British Fund for keeping Basutos, Pondos, Zulus quiet?" Australians, we have seen, offered to do this very thing. But it is only up to a certain stage of early growth, that large Colonies require external help from other parts of the Empire to maintain order among their aboriginal population. New Zealand needed it twenty years ago. She will never require it again, because her British population is now large enough to cope with all native and other difficulties arising within the Colony. South Africa would, in like manner, soon be able to manage her provincial affairs, if she could increase her European population by a large influx of people from England. These native questions can be much better settled by British emigrants than by British soldiers.

Mr. Morley also has doubts as to Colonies not directly concerned in the questions taking part against the

French, in order to maintain Australian interests in the Pacific, or British North American fishery rights on the coasts of Newfoundland. Surely, upon no higher principle than that known in America as "log-rolling," Canadians and Australians would find it to their interest to support each other against foreign nations, whose interference in their waters, and probably in their territories, might become very serious if Canada and Australia were independent. But Mr. Morley prophesies that "it would be a *mandat impératif* on every federal delegate not to vote a penny for any war, or preparation of war, that might arise from the direct or indirect interests of any Colony but his own." If this were so, the Peace-at-any-price Party ought to become Imperial Federalists. But here, again, experience is dead against Mr. Morley. We have never heard of a *mandat impératif* from the Pacific or Midland States of America against "any war or preparation of war," or any policy exclusively affecting the interests of the Eastern States; and when this country has within recent years been almost on the verge of war, the Colonies have either felt that their interests were involved with those of the Mother Country in the questions at issue, or that the honour of the Empire was at stake; for, although war would have seriously compromised them, no protests against it came from them; on the contrary, they prepared not only to defend themselves, but also, as we have seen, made offers of aid to this country. With federation, national sentiment and prestige would be sufficient to secure the cheerful co-operation of all our dominions—those who might have no direct interest in the question at issue in one war feeling that when their turn came to be attacked or menaced, they would be able to command the whole power of the Empire. But, as Mr. Service has expressed the idea, " a great Britannic Empire " would be " permanent and peaceful " — peaceful because permanent and powerful. Many questions affecting our joint and several interests will never be raised by foreign nations if we stand together, and the world will never have to deplore many wars which will otherwise occur. If union be strength, strength means peace for·us, and disunion weakness, the multiplication of national divisions, jealousies, and wars. Strong powers are less liable to be attacked, and they have no need to wage wars to show that they are not afraid to fight.

Mr. Morley supposes that " the Federal Council would be deliberative and executive," and wants to know " whence its executive would be taken." Those who cannot, or will not, see their way to British federation are always raising difficulties about a " Federal Council." They have to be repeatedly reminded that there is no such thing in existence as federal government by a mere council, all the existing federations having Parliaments, with two Chambers and executives, and, *à fortiori*, the greater federation of Great Britain could not ultimately do with less. At the thought that, if the Federal Cabinet and Council became supreme, " the mother of Parliaments would sink into the condition of a State legislature," Mr. Morley's strongest conservatism seems stirred within him. Does he not, however, like the present so-called Imperial Parliament best when it is discharging, the functions of a State legislature? A division of labour, whereby it would hand over Imperial affairs[1] to a

[1] As to its retaining Imperial, and handing over Provincial , affairs, see pages 69, 196.

Parliament of the Empire, might enable it to get through the increasing work of legislating for the British Isles, with which it is now so much over-burdened ; and it would be a great gain to have foreign policy taken out of the arena of the party contentions of this country. On the assumption that their representatives would range themselves on opposite sides, the alternative dilemma of this country or the Colonies being supreme in the " Council," is next suggested, and that, in the former event, on the part of the Colonies, " the same resentment and sense of grievance which was in the old times directed against the centralization of the Colonial Office, would instantly revive against the centralization of the new council." As if the centralization which formerly regulated the local affairs of Australia from Downing Street, could be compared with that centralization whereby the common concerns, and external relations of an empire must necessarily be directed from its capital !

Then it is contended by Mr. Morley that, as it was so difficult to form a federation in Canada, and that as Australia has not yet succeeded in founding one, the obstacles to the establishment of a Federal Union of the Empire would be " enormous." Now a moment's reflection, as to the nature of Intercolonial Federation and Imperial Federation, will suffice to show that the difficulties in the way of the former are much more numerous and considerable than those in the way of the latter. The question of the capital and of pre-cedence, which are formidable in considering Inter-colonial Federation, would only have to be mentioned to be unanimously decided in favour of the old country in arranging an Imperial Federation; and many questions which Colonies must give up to federal control in an Intercolonial Federal Union, would be retained by them as purely provincial or inter-provincial on entering into an Imperial Federation. The late Mr. William Forster, of New South Wales, in his able paper on " The Fallacies of Federation," [1] whilst arguing against and pointing out the difficulties of Intercolonial Federation, expressed himself in favour of Imperial Federation.

That the territories of existing federations are conterminous, whilst those of ours would be separated by oceans, is assumed by Mr. Morley and other Anti-Federalists to be to our disadvantage. But Professor Thorold Rogers, in his Cobden Club Essay, some years ago, when our constantly improving means of communication were not nearly as advanced as they are at present, disposed of this *occanus dissociabilis* objection. There is room, moreover, for contending that the separation of territories by seas may facilitate, rather than retard, their federal union; for the ocean will at once define what interests and questions are federal and what provincial, whereas if the territories are adjacent their concerns often so overlap each other that many questions cannot be left to provincial control. But with the ocean intervening, the relations of our Empire would be more clear and simple, greater freedom of action being left to the provinces, without the federal government being less powerful for the general defence or less effective for the direction of the common concerns of the Empire.

Mr. Morley puts the question very clearly when he says: " If we can both persuade ourselves and convince the Colonists that the gains of a closer confederation will compensate for the sacrifices entailed by it,

---

[1] *Proceedings of the Royal Colonial Institute*, vol. viii. p. 79.

we shall then look at the problem with the same eyes; if not, not." What would be the sacrifices? For England, they would only amount to taking the Colonies into partnership, and giving them a voice in the joint concerns and external policies of her Empire; and if this should involve the creation of a new Imperial Parliament, and the turning of the present one into a more efficient provincial legislature for these isles, there would be a real gain, more than making up for any sentimental sacrifices; for as Prussia is greater in federal Germany, so would England be in federal Great Britain. She would, for all purposes of national strength, make permanently her own the growing wealth and increasing British population— already nearly ten millions — of Greater Britain. Against such a gain a mere sentimental sacrifice, or even a substantial sacrifice, if either had to be made, would weigh but little. Besides, the loss of the Colonies—of whose fortified harbours and coaling-stations she now has full use without cost to her— would entail upon her taxpayers the heavy extra burden, of forming and maintaining other places of refuge and resort for the fleets and cruisers she would require, to protect her mercantile marine and commerce—if these should remain long with her after the disintegration of her Empire. Diplomatic relations with the Colonies, if independent, would also cost her much; and their ports would have to extend the hospitalities of neutrality to her foes in time of war.

And what would the Colonies have to sacrifice? Absolutely nothing which they have at present. They would give up the prospect of figuring before the world in the isolation of independence. They would forego the vain importance of spreading separate networks of diplomatic relations among the nations, whereby the number of their foreign policies, and the complications of human affairs, would be so much increased that wars and rumours of wars would much more abound. Even if there were "the want of national spirit" of the provincial type, which Professor Goldwin Smith imagines and deplores, there would be a far better, broader, more enlightened, national spirit—unbounded by the limits of provinces and dominions, or by the expanse of oceans, and as world-wide in the range of its sympathies as the race and Empire of Great Britain. The Provincial, or Intercolonial Federal Parliaments of the Colonies, would as completely retain control of their domestic concerns as the Parliament of the British Isles would of theirs. The Colonies might have to place some of their defensive works and forces under Imperial, naval, and military control, and in common with the British Isles, to have a small percentage of their taxes levied by the Federal Parliament. But the amount would be a fraction of what they would have to pay, if they had separately to provide for their own defences, and it would be a decreasing percentage, in ratio with the increase of wealth and population throughout the Empire.[1]

Mr. Morley concludes by speaking of the Federalists "aiming at an artificial centralization"—whatever he may mean by that, seeing that they advocate the complete provincial control of local affairs; he suggests that the "ideal is a great Roman Empire which shall be capable, by means of fleets and armies, of imposing its will upon the world"; and, with that confidence of assertion which runs through the entire

[1] See page 184.

article—even when the views of such men as Professor Seeley and Mr. Forster are being disposed of and Colonial experience ignored—we are told in its last words that " the ideal is as impracticable as it is puerile and retrograde." Of course the idea of a great modern Roman Empire is absurd; but it is desirable that the British Empire—though its policy and influences would be pacific—should weld together and be able to wield its great strength, not only for the defence of its own interests, but also for the furtherance of peace and justice in the world. Mr. Goldwin Smith bewails the fact that England has acquired India, and must retain and govern that country. Her commerce, as much as her Oriental dependency, make the Suez Canal and Egypt of great importance to her. Australia, and also Canada, with her large, increasing, mercantile marine, must be much interested in them both. Greater Britain ought, therefore, to be summoned to the aid of Great Britain, to maintain these and other common national interests and responsibilities. The people, and statesmen of this brave little island, may well fear to see her overtax her strength, by attempting single-handed to bear fresh responsibilities, which would press but lightly upon her if borne in conjunction with her robust Colonial children. Although it would not be to the interests of the Empire as a whole, and seldom of any of its dominions, to undertake aggressive wars, still our obligations to humanity and civilization might require us to do so. Take such an instance as that now before us—the case of the Soudan. Our selfish Imperial national interests might dictate that we should not interfere in that country; but, if there were no danger of our overtaxing our strength by a fresh enterprise, the best thing which we could do for the wretched Soudanese, even if we had to do it by war and conquest, would be to crush the infamous slave-trade and organize among them a rule of peace, justice, and liberty. But, some Englishmen distrust their country; their sympathies seem always with her foes or rivals, be they white or black, civilized or uncivilized; they appear to wish that she should be weak rather than strong, that her power should not be increased, lest it should be used for evil instead of for good. To them, the prospect of Imperial Federation may well seem appalling.

Mr. Morley praises as "a masterpiece of brilliant style and finished dialectics" Mr. Goldwin Smith's work, "The Empire," in which that negation of a policy—disintegration—was advocated more than twenty years ago; and since the appearance of the article by the former gentleman one by the latter has been published. This is really an abbreviated, but not less lachrymose edition, of the famous lamentations of Professor Goldwin Smith over the existence and condition of the Empire. Two decades have passed since they appeared; and though shadows which hung over our Colonial prospects—notably in Canada and New Zealand—have long cleared away, Mr. Smith is gloomy still; and though many of his anticipations of disaster and evil have been shown, by Colonial progress, to have been groundless, he is as confident as ever in "the conviction of at least one English-man." He starts with an inaccurate assertion, that "Imperialism regards all the parts of the motley heritage—the Colonies, India, and the military dependencies alike, as portions of an Empire not less inalienable than Kent." The advocates of permanent unity, whilst prepared to give up none of the dominions of the Empire, maintain that the bonds of kindred between the Mother Country and the Colonies must ever make their union much more sacred than that with any alien race. Mr. Smith gives his version of the history of the expansion of England as opposed to that of Mr. Seeley. He regards the acquisition of India as an evil from which there is no escape. "It is enough," so he puts it, "to task the governing powers of an Imperial country, even if it were not, as it certainly is, bringing Egypt in its train;" and "of withdrawal, at all events, nobody now thinks." A patriotic philosopher, oppressed with the conviction that his country must endure such burdens, ought surely to strain every argument to secure for her any possible support, to convince the Colonies that they are only expansions of England—so many "Kents;" he ought surely to be among the foremost of Imperial Federalists. Malta is the only place to the retention of which Mr. Smith sees no objection; he favours the exchange of Gibraltar for Ceuta; and, as to the West Indies, "it would have been more profitable to buy their sugar than to possess them," for the "connection would be most onerous and dangerous in case of war."

Coming next to the Colonies proper, Mr. Goldwin Smith challenges, as he does in the last words of his postscript, the Federalists to produce some practical plan; just as if federation were a mere speculative idea instead of a well-tried system of government, the success of which has been proved upon both large and small scales. Like other opponents,[1] he thinks to stifle the question with a string of interrogatories, upon points of detail, which have been already adjusted in

[1] See page 205.

the construction of existing Federal Governments.
For instance, as to who should be included, the
distribution of representation, the relations of the
Federal Government with that of this country, where
it would be seated, as to advantages and disadvantages
to the old and new countries; and with these questions
are mingled abundant assertions, for instance, as to
the impossibility of believing that the Colonies would
do what they would never be asked to do—"consent
to surrender their power of self-taxation, to allow their
tariffs to be regulated by an assembly in London;"
and then there are the old objections about the
unwillingness of the Colonies to take part in wars,
and of England to "allow her foreign policy to be
controlled by Colonial politicians"—as if these would
combine against the old country, and our interests be
divided by sectional lines, and be in rivalry instead
of being national and imperial. Doubts are even
expressed as to a "Conference for framing the Federal
Constitution" being possible, although we have also
instances of the success of conferences for such
purposes.[1]

Now, the position of the Federalists is a strong one.
They have proposed no new expedient, nor do they
claim credit for having invented any original theory
of government; but they point to practical experience,
and ask that trial may be made—on a more extended
scale, no doubt—of a system which, so far as it has yet
been applied, has proved the life and strength of great
nations. They appeal to what has been done, and say
it can be done again—leaving their opponents only
the ground of assertion and prediction to stand upon,
to affirm the inability of Englishmen—who have

[1] See further on, page 225.

hitherto been famed for the ease with which they have adapted their institutions to their expanding national needs—to apply the federal system to their Empire. It is also open to the Anti-Federalists to prophesy that the oceans, which are becoming more and more the highways of our dominions, will prove insuperable barriers to their continued political union.

Mr. Goldwin Smith attempts to make a point of the fact that "Federationists bewail British ignorance of the Colonies," which, he asserts, "denotes an absence of community of interest which would be fatal to Federation." It might as well be said that the difference of interests and ideas between an urban and rural population, in this or any country, is incompatible with their union in one state. It is, doubtless, most desirable that the people of all parts of the Empire should know as much as possible about each other, and that such knowledge should be extensively imparted in all their schools; but as a Federal Government would have to deal with general, not with provincial, interests, the members of the Parliament of the Empire would be sufficiently acquainted with its Imperial wants and interests; they would have as much in common with respect to these, as the members for Caithness and for Cornwall have with respect to the affairs of this island.

"In war," says Mr. Smith, "England would have to defend the Colonies," as they would not "consent to maintain a standing army or navy;" and this statement is made notwithstanding the fact that the Canadians, with their militia—which even Mr. Smith computes at forty thousand strong—and the Australians with their harbour fortifications and vessels, have done and are doing much to strengthen their defences. We are also told—and the following assertions show how those who find fault with everything are inconsistent with themselves—that "it is hard to see how these distant dependencies can be other than sources of military weakness to England;" but that it is only from "their connection with her and her Imperial diplomacy, and from that alone, that their liability to be involved in war arises;" and that, as "territorial rapacity does not exist in the United States," that Republic is not in the least "disposed to aggress upon Canada." From whence, then, can the Dominion—the only portion of the Colonial Empire on the same mainland with any great Power—be a source of "military weakness" to England, unless she and the States unexpectedly develop a disposition to quarrel? Is Russia or any other Power likely to march an army across the Pacific to invade Canada, or in like manner to attack Australia or South Africa? If these latter dominions cannot be reached by any overland expedition, and if the chance of Canada being thus attacked from the United States is so extremely remote, it is only by stretching improbabilities to the uttermost that the Colonial Empire can be said to be, and that only in one direction, a possible source of "military weakness" to the Mother Country. That—with their fine harbours, fortified ports, increasing marine population—the Colonies could soon, with Imperial Federation and an organized system of defences, become a source of enormous strength to England and each other, needs no space to demonstrate. But, only three pages beyond the paragraph which begins with the statement that "England would have to defend the Colonies," and goes on to say that they would be "sources of military weakness," Mr. Smith tells us that

" Australia lies in an ocean by herself, she entangles England in no liabilities or responsibilities beyond the possible necessity of protecting her in a maritime war." Disruptionists, in trying to prove the weakness occasioned by each portion of the Empire to the others, only succeed in showing how important it is for them all to be bound together for the sake of combined strength. Reasons which are assigned to England in favour of disintegration may be arguments against it for the Colonies, and *vice versâ;* in short, disintegrationists only state to the one the advantages to the other of continuing the union, and flatter themselves that they are demonstrating its inutility.

Nothing could be more doleful than the picture which Mr. Goldwin Smith draws of the evils occasioned by " the complete want of national spirit in the Colonies." The astounding statement is made that " no pride is felt in the country," that " the very productions of a dependency are apt to be rated low by its own people." Such passages reveal a depth of pessimist despondency, which clearly accounts for the distorted vision with which the writer views the entire relations of the Empire. Having been born and brought up in Australia, I am bound, for once in this article, to speak in the first person, in order to testify that what is described is totally at variance with everything I have felt myself, or have known of the feelings of others with regard to that country, and of all I have ever heard from Canadians and South Africans respecting their portions of the Empire. Mr. Anthony Trollope has described Colonists as given to " blowing," or boasting of themselves and their country; and there is more fear of young communities, like young people, thinking too much instead of too

little of themselves.   Lover of old England and strong
Imperialist though I am, it has always been my pride
to own Australia as the land of my birth, and to avow
that she possesses my strongest affections.   All these
feelings perfectly harmonize; for, if I may be pardoned
for quoting what I wrote some time ago,[1]—"the highest
perfection, the most complete greatness of which any
Colony, or even the Mother Country herself, is capable,
is not to be found in the isolation of single communities, or even of great groups of States, but in
the unity of a common Empire, whose magnificent
territories stretch into every clime and quarter of
the globe, and whose combined strength will, with
the blessing of God, be a sure guarantee of security
and peace to the weakest as well as the strongest
member of that Empire."   Or, as Sir Henry Parkes
so well puts it—after picturing the greatness which
Australia must achieve if she were to become an
independent Power—"She would miss her higher
destiny, her rightful share in what may be a more
glorious rule than mankind has ever yet seen;" and
"to be included in a Confederation, so all-powerful
and beneficent, is what my feeble voice would claim
for Australia."

In Mr. Smith's expression of general dissatisfaction
with everything, it is only to be expected that the
office of Colonial Governor, and especially Governor-
General of Canada, should be included.   What harm
it has done may be estimated by the statement that,
"If Canada had a chance of becoming a nation independent of the United States, she owes the loss of it,
in no small measure, to a governor-general of the

[1] In the conclusion to my "Early History of the Colony of
Victoria."

more active kind." If this be recognized as a fact,
great as the services of Lord Dufferin are acknowledged to have been, it will constitute his chief claim
to the lasting gratitude of the people of the Dominion,
as well as of the whole Empire. The Canadian
Pacific Railway, and the Federation itself, do not
escape the universal censure upon all things connected
with the Colonies and India in which Professor Smith
indulges.

The dead cause of disintegration is not likely to
be galvanized into life, by the combined efforts and
ability of Mr. John Morley, Professor Goldwin Smith,
and Mr. Frederic Harrison. These and other able
writers may try their best to stem the rising tide of
material interest and national sentiment, which already
runs so high, both in this country and the Colonies,
against any further severance or division of the British
race. The spirit of national unity has been one of
the most beneficent influences in the enlightened
progress of modern times. It has made Italy; it has
made Germany. An opposite tendency will not un-
make England. She will not submit herself to the
shrivelling prescriptions of an insular philosophy.
National magnetism, with the power of a loadstone,
is drawing together Great and Greater Britain in
closer indissoluble union. The maintenance of that
union is the highest political object for England and
for the Colonies. It is a national policy. It ought
never to be made a party question, save only in so
far as the opposite sides in our Parliaments should
vie with each other in producing the best means of
giving it effect. It is truly Conservative, for what
is better worth conserving than our Empire from
disintegration? It is Liberal in the best sense of the

term, for what can be more liberal and enlightened than the idea of maintaining the brotherhood of the British race—of keeping the people of England and of the Colonies, of all creeds and classes, nationally united, never to be aliens to each other?

If union be desirable for the sake of strength, and strength for the sake of security and peace, our Empire will ultimately need to be organized on a permanent basis, with a Federal Government not less efficient than those of some of the greatest Powers to which the Empire of Great Britain will not be inferior. There will surely not be a dearth of states-men in our expanded territories, and increasing popu-lations, to provide such an organization as soon as it may be required. In the mean time, it behoves the people of the Empire to keep the question well in view; for the rapid growth of the Colonies is propel-ling us towards Federation, at a speed which is fast awakening general recognition.

CHAPTER IX.

MARKING PROGRESS AND DEVELOPMENT.

Progress in fifteen years from 1869—Position of the Colonial
Empire in that year—How New Zealand became able to
manage her internal affairs—Duty of Parent State to Infant
Colony—Rapid establishment of Canadian Federation and
Australasian self-government—Express speed of Colonial
progress—Leading men favourable to Unity of Empire—
Lord Norton and "Imperial Federation; Its Impossibility"
—Colonial growth does not admit of slow growth of institutions—Age of Colony of Victoria shows this—When single
Parliament and Executive can manage domestic and external
affairs—Federation indispensable for United States of America
and United Empire of Great Britain—Resolutions of Conference on Imperial Federation of 1884—Federalists need not
propose detailed Constitution—For governments to do this—
What Federal Government has done for nations that have
adopted it—English Parliament giving up control of foreign
affairs—Entanglement of foreign questions with domestic
party politics—Division of labour—Colonies submitting to
Imperial taxation—Mr. Service on their bearing expense of
defences—Interests in common—Differences of Fiscal policy
—Amount of products of United Kingdom taken by Protectionist Victoria.—Lighter taxation—Co-operative defence—
Peace—Effects of war—For England and the Colonies to stand
alone—Feeling towards United States—No further division
of British race.

The consideration of the question having so far
advanced, I felt it would be profitable to note progress made, so availing myself of an invitation to
bring the subject before the Social Science Congress
at Birmingham, on September 19th, 1884, I read a
paper which, with a few omissions, to avoid repetitions

in this work, forms the present chapter. I explained at the outset that, as one of the Honorary Secretaries of the provisional committee for organizing the new Federation Society, I did not appear in any representative capacity, but was alone responsible for this utterance.

At the Bristol Congress of this Association, in 1869, England and her Colonies formed the subject of a discussion which was opened by three or four papers—one of these being my first on the question. The fifteen years which have since elapsed seem an age in the growth of everything which the energy of our people has been planting and cultivating in the new lands of Great Britain. Progress—social, political, commercial, educational, locomotive, telegraphic—has marked the period, and has led to a condition of things between England and the Colonies satisfactory beyond all the hopes and anticipations of those of us who, in 1869, were firm believers in and decided advocates of, the permanent unity of the Empire.

What was the position of the Colonial Empire at the time of the Bristol discussion? Briefly this— Affairs in New Zealand were then the chief source of anxiety, doubts being seriously entertained whether, on the withdrawal of the Imperial troops, the Colonists would be able to hold their own against the Maoris. The wise introduction, however, of a stream of emigration from this country soon increased the population of the Colony so as speedily and for ever to settle that question, and to enable New Zealand to manage her own internal affairs without needing further aid from this country. It may be asked, in passing, if a similar influx from the teeming population of this island into South Africa might not also prove a peaceful solution of the difficulties of that country, and cause that, in a few years, its present troubles shall also be matters of the past.

Experience abundantly proves that Colonies, after requiring, during a few years of infantine weakness, the support of the Mother Country, may grow, not only able to manage their own internal affairs, but to bear a share in maintaining the strength and defensive power of the Empire. The parent would be unnatural and cruel, as well as unwise, to grudge a short period of trouble and expense in tending offspring who were certain to repay, with interest, the cost of their early rearing. What may be true of parent and child is more certain to be so of parent State and offspring Colony, for death in the former instance must intervene to prevent the benefit of the relationship being perpetual.[1]

It is difficult to realize, that fifteen years ago that great and successful Federation, which has given to Canada the appearance and substantial advantages of a matured and long-settled State, had not come into existence. In Australasia, also, constitutional self-government had then only entered its teens, for it was but thirteen years old—1856 having been the year of its establishment in almost all the Colonies at the Antipodes. Telegraphic communication with them had not been opened, nor had the great Canadian Pacific Railway, which will so soon be completed, been commenced. The importance of New Guinea to the Empire, or to Australia, was not then thought of. One of the first times that it was suggested was in a paper by Mr. Westgarth, at the Plymouth Congress of this Association, in 1872. A British Protectorate

[1] See page 37.

has just been established in the island.   So rapidly
do questions spring up and ripen, that they require
the constant watchfulness and the timely handling of
the rulers of the Empire.

The slightest sketch of the developments of Colonial
questions and policies must demonstrate the importance
of looking well before us when—with the ever-increasing
express speed of modern and especially of Colonial
progress—we find ourselves hurrying into the future,
with its still more numerous growths, and larger and
more rapid developments, of questions and policies.
Most men of intelligence and observation, like that
rising statesman Lord Rosebery, usually return from
visiting any of the leading groups of Colonies deeply
impressed with the conviction, that the unity of the
Empire should be permanently maintained.   Among
the strongest advocates of this policy are those who
know the Colonies longest and best, and have seen
most of their early growth—eminent men like Sir
Alexander Galt, Sir John Macdonald, Sir Henry
Parkes, Mr. Service, Sir Julius Vogel, and also one of
the ablest and most experienced of Colonial Governors,
Sir Hercules Robinson.   Lord Norton differs from these
and other weighty authorities; but his ideas of the
relations with the Colonies seem to date from a period
of official connection with them in Downing Street,
when they were in a state of mere infancy.   Those
who can only conceive of them in that condition will
agree with " Imperial Federation : Its Impossibility,"
in the *Nineteenth Century Review* for September, 1884.
A representative public man from an important Colony
recently remarked to me that Imperial Federation had
been brought " within the range of practical politics."
To say that a question is outside that range may be

a convenient mode of disposing of it, for those who lack
either the taste or the capacity for dealing with great
and important considerations. But the investigation
of no question bearing upon the future of our growing
Empire can safely be said to be unpractical. The
speculations of yesterday are the urgent questions of
to-day, which will have to be settled to-morrow.
Modern Colonial growth does not tarry to admit of
the slow development, however desirable, of such
institutions as may be required either for the regulation
of the internal affairs of Colonies, or of their relations
with each other, or with the Mother Country. Men
still live whose memories stretch beyond the half
century—which, to-day, wants exactly two months of
being complete—since the Henty brothers, the first
permanent white settlers, landed on what is now the
Colony of Victoria, with its population of nine hundred
thousand. Even I can remember seeing, when a child,
the goats grazing on what are now some of the leading
streets of its capital, Melbourne. I distinctly recollect
when Victoria, the Port Philip district of New South
Wales, was formed into a separate Crown Colony,
and when the question of its having responsible
self-government came within the range of practical
politics, just thirty years ago. No wonder that
any one remembering such things should feel strongly
that this question of Imperial organization or Federation
is sure rapidly to ripen.

It will matter little what the organization may be
called if it give a sufficient voice in the management,
and a fair share of the burden of our common concerns,
to all our dominions. The common central authority
would have to utilize the common resources of the
Empire, to gather up its strength for the defence of all

its members, to regulate its relations with foreign
States, to manage all its affairs which are not Provincial
or Interprovincial, to raise from all its territories the
revenues required for such purposes. Any authority
performing such functions must be a Federal authority,
unless no Provincial Parliaments were in existence,
and the power of legislating both for Provincial
and Imperial purposes were centred in one general
Parliament. Within certain limits it is possible for
a single Parliament and Executive satisfactorily to
perform the double functions of managing the domestic
and the external affairs of a nation ; but when a people
extends over a vast territory like the United States
it is impossible for a single Government efficiently to
legislate for, and administer the multitudinous concerns
and interests of millions of men. Provincial government for local affairs, and Federal government for
general and external concerns, are therefore indispensable to perfect organization. The very national
life of our American kinsmen depends upon such an
arrangement. They might, of course, with a want
of spirit and energy—the opposite of their character
—have been content with an impotent policy of
disorganization, disintegration, division, contraction,
which a few very insular philosophers recommend
to England as her wisest Colonial policy. Nothing
short, however, of suicidal mania is likely to induce
her to inflict upon herself the mutilations they advise
—the amputation of some of the stoutest limbs of her
Empire.

If Provincial self-government and Federal government be necessary for the United States of America,
à fortiori, they will be so for the future United Empire
of Great Britain. At the Conference on Imperial

Federation, on July 29, 1884, it was unanimously resolved—" 1. That in order to secure the permanent unity of the Empire some form of Federation is essential." " 2. That for the purpose of influencing public opinion, both in the United Kingdom and the Colonies, by showing the incalculable advantages which will accrue to the whole Empire from the adoption of such a system of organization, a society be formed of men of all parties to advocate and support the principle of Federation." This is the deliberate conclusion of one of the most important gatherings of distinguished Colonists, and English Members of Parliament, of all shades of opinion.

Imperial Federation was barely mentioned at the Bristol Congress of 1869, the Colonies not having then sufficiently emerged from infancy to admit of its consideration. Before the remaining fifteen years of the century have expired, it will probably be established, at least in an elementary form. But what must the complete organization be? Federalists are sometimes challenged to go into details, and to produce a Constitution. They would not be the practical men they are if they were to do anything of the kind. They would be acting as if they were mere theorists, proposing something which had never been tried by the test of being practically worked, and which consequently could only be explained by being elaborately drawn out upon paper. Every well-informed man knows what Federal government is— that it is a well-tried and efficient system; that without it the United States would not be; that it has delivered Germany from the liability to be divided and governed by a Napoleon; that it has saved the Austrian Empire from being broken in pieces; that it has made the Dominion of Canada, and enabled the different races of Switzerland to remain united for mutual protection, when without it, even in so small a territory, they could not have held together as a free and independent State.

As the *Minutes of the Views of the Committee* presented to the recent Conference puts it, "the details" of Imperial Federation should be "left to be adjusted by those authoritatively empowered to arrange them on behalf of this country and the Colonies, when the time shall arrive for the formation of such Federation;" all that is now needed being that "the nature and different forms of Federal Government" at present working in the world be sufficiently considered, "so that the people of the Empire, both in these isles and beyond the seas, may be better able to decide as to the exact form of that Government which they may prefer whenever they shall feel that the time has arrived for its adoption."

It has been objected that Imperial Federation could not be carried out unless the present British Parliament were to hand over to a new Parliament, representing the whole Empire, the control of foreign[1] affairs and general defence. If this be so, the division of labour which would be thus effected would in itself compensate the old country, for giving the new countries of the Empire a share in the management of Imperial affairs; for then the British Isles would have a Parliament of their own exclusively devoted to their domestic concerns, to which, from overpressure of work, and attention divided between home and Imperial affairs, the present Parliament cannot give the time demanded. The entanglements of foreign and domestic questions

[1] Pages 20, 53, 68, 158.

would no longer be possible, to the great relief of many reflecting men, who may often feel their sympathies divided between the political parties on these questions. It would also, for other reasons, be a great national gain if foreign affairs were placed beyond the contentions of domestic party politics. England would gain far more than she would give up by taking the Colonies into partnership in the government of the Empire; for the national security would be placed beyond doubt, without the burdens of the taxpayers of the British Isles being increased. They would, on the contrary, be lightened, for a fair share of representation extended to all parts of the Empire would be attended with the constitutional obligation to contribute to the Imperial revenue, which, for co-operative defence, would be a much lighter burden on all the people of the Empire than separate taxation for separate defence.

But objectors will perhaps assert that the Colonies would not submit to taxation, even if they had representation.[1] Canada and Australia have, however, repeatedly shown their disposition to help the Mother Country. The Australian Colonies have just taxed themselves for an Imperial purpose—the establishment of British authority in New Guinea—although they are to have no control over the expenditure of the money they have voted. And what did Mr. Service, the Premier of Victoria, say in his speech, made June 19th, 1884, when he carried the Assembly of the Colony unanimously with him in his policy? Speaking of defences, beyond those of their coasts and harbours, which the Colonies themselves maintain, the words of Mr. Service were : " Why should the people

[1] See pages 92, 96, 162, 199.

of England bear the cost of protecting us? . . . In the more infancy of Colonies, it is right and proper for England to spread her wings over them, and to enable them to grow up without foreign intervention until they are able to protect themselves; but that we who are placed in a prosperous part of the world—prosperous far beyond our fellow-countrymen in England—should desire for one moment to take money out of their pockets when we can spare it far better out of our own is a thing, at all events at this day, no Australian will contend for." There is the right Imperial ring, the true Federal spirit, sounded forth by a Colonial statesman, who not long ago expressed the hope that he might yet sit in this country, in some legislative body which should represent the whole Empire.

It is sometimes asked, with little thought, What interests [1] have this country, Canada, and Australasia in common, that they should stand together and support each other, perhaps at the risk of getting into wars? In the Pacific Ocean alone their great and growing commercial and political interests are already identical. They all will become more and more interested in the Suez Canal and the questions affecting it. That important highway to this country from Australia, will practically be the only trade route from the latter into the Mediterranean, as the ramifications of her commerce become more extended. Mr. Dalton has shown that, commercially, Australia and Canada are already almost as much interested in Belgium as England is, and that they promise at no distant date to be so to a greater extent.

It is sometimes asserted that differences of fiscal

[1] Pages 130, 198.

policy, about which all communities may, perhaps, never think alike, must be fatal to our Federal Union. But tariffs do not even now interfere with the good relations between the members of the Empire. Victoria, the most protectionist of Colonies, takes £12 5s. 2d. per head of her population, of the productions of this country. New South Wales adheres to free trade, and so do most of the other Colonies. Canada indulges in a mild form of protection. But if the protectionist Colonies were to enter an Imperial Federation, retaining their provincial tariffs, that would not prevent them from adding materially to the strength of the Union; and they would be the more likely, of their own free will, to abandon duties restrictive of trade with their fellow-subjects than if, by separation, these fellow-subjects were to be made foreigners to them. Restrictions to trade, more incompatible with national unity than any imposed by Colonial tariffs, fettered the commercial relations of the people of this single island not so many years back.

The organized unity of the Empire means, in the future, lighter taxation, greater efficiency, economy of defence, and absolute security for this country and for the Colonies. Upon both, separation—a thing as much treason to our people as to our Sovereign—would entail as great additional expense as the difference between indifferent, and costly isolated defence and perfect but cheap co-operative defence.

There is one policy, one interest of the many we have in common, which is above all others supreme, and that is the maintenance of peace. War, however victoriously we might come out of it, must at best be an enormous evil to the whole British people, both in these isles and beyond the seas. But it is not to be avoided, rather to be courted, by any national indications that we are prepared to submit to anything rather than enter into it. An unsuccessful maritime war would be destructive to the old country and to the Colonies; it would stop the looms of Lancashire, extinguish the furnaces of Birmingham, and blight Colonial growth; it would raise provisions in this country, which are so largely imported, to siege prices. Even in a war successful to us, cruisers would, with ten times the destruction of the *Alabama* and *Shenandoah*, sweep our merchant-ships from the ocean.

Till better influences prevail in the world, to an extent which they have never attained at any period of human history, unhappily, one of the wisest and most practical ways of avoiding war will be to be prepared for it. Mr. Cobden—one of the greatest friends of peace and commerce—was in favour of maintaining a powerful British navy. Mr. Childers said, five years ago, that that navy should be equal to the combined fleets of any three other Powers. For England to stand alone, and for the Colonies to be independent, and to maintain efficient naval defences to safeguard their interests as great Powers, would require that each should keep up " bloated armaments," for which their taxpayers would be heavily burdened. But by combining their strength in joint co-operative defence, fewer war-ships and fighting men, and much lighter taxes, will suffice to ensure the security and the power of a united British people. A strong man is less likely to be provoked into a fight than one doubtful of his strength; the biggest boy is seldom the bully of the school; even the Newfoundland dog can, without loss of dignity, remain pacific under provocation. The United Empire of Great Britain, armed upon the ocean—far within the capabilities of its increasing wealth and population to bear defensive arming—would be so strong that all its dominions could pursue their internal development conscious of the security of a joint protection, and their external commerce would be at peace. "When a strong man armed keepeth his palace, his goods are at peace." So would it be with our strong United Empire. Good will and friendship with other nations should not be the less our policy; we should seek to "live peaceably with all men." But foreigners may misunderstand us —may regard us with jealousy, be fickle in their esteem of us—alliances with them may fail us. The constancy of the affection of our own race and nation must, then, be our consolation. There is one great people whose interests, ideas and sympathies run parallel with our own, whose welfare we should ever desire, whose national unity we should hope may, like ours, be for ever preserved—a people who, if wisdom had presided in our councils a century ago, might have continued one with us—our near kinsmen across the Atlantic. We were, unhappily, divided from them by a policy the reverse of that which has long been cementing the unity of our parent State and offspring communities.[1]

Our great principle is that there shall be no further division of the British people. May God forbid it! Our greatest policy is the organization of our union for the mutual security, happiness, and peace of all its members, for the attainment by them all, both collectively and severally, of the highest perfection of which they are capable. That perfection is to be found in their organized union, not in their being split into sections, not in their disintegration and isolation.

[1] See pages 43, 47, 145, 213.

CHAPTER X.

ESSENTIAL PRINCIPLES OF BRITISH FEDERATION.

Mr. Forster and "the idea realizing itself"—Imperial Federalists not pledged to details, but desire discussion of various schemes—Professional critics—Federalists do not propose Constitutions—Present relations—Sentiment without organization—No feasible scheme?—Combination "on an equitable basis"—Equitable representation—Position of India—Imperial taxation—Self-governing Colonies to retain complete control of their Provincial affairs—Temporary expedients—Imperial Parliament and Ministry—Present Imperial Parliament might become that of Empire—Distinct one would be required for Provincial affairs of British Isles—Our common interests, everywhere—Basis of strength of Great Powers—Sir Alexander Stuart on raising an Imperial revenue—Suggestions of Sir Alexander Galt and Mr. Thos. Macfarlane—Mr. Hofmeyr's proposal at Colonial Conference—Annual cost of Naval construction—Objection to subsidies.

On the next occasion, when called on to open a discussion of the question, it occurred to me that it would be useful to define the principles which must form the basis of all Federal unions whatever may be the details of their organizations. This chapter, therefore, formed the contents of my paper read at the opening of the series of conferences, held under the auspices of the Royal Colonial Institute, at the Colonial and Indian Exhibition, on May 28th, 1886.

The Duke of Manchester occupied the chair, and, in opening the proceedings, said: "In recent speeches of distinguished persons, references have been made to the Federation of the Empire. The idea has been advocated in the most eloquent terms, and, from the tone of the speakers, one might suppose they had imbibed the idea with their mother's milk. It is most gratifying to those who started the idea, and who have constantly advocated it, to find that it has taken such a hold on the public mind ; but I think we should all have been pleased—we who advocated the Federation of the Empire originally, and in the face of considerable ridicule—I say we should all have been pleased had some recognition been made of those first efforts. Still, we are gratified with the results, and I am sure no one more so than one of the most energetic advocates of this policy—Mr. Labilliere—whom I will now ask to read a paper on the subject."

It was as follows :—Had a text been required for my subject to-day, I should have chosen words of that great and, throughout the length and breadth of the Empire, most popular of statesmen, whose recent death has created an irreparable blank in the many gatherings of this Colonial Exhibition season—where his presence would have been so welcome, and his voice would have been heard with so much interest and approbation. The words of Mr. Forster to which I refer occur in his famous Edinburgh address—which gave such powerful expression to the principle of the Unity of the Empire—where it is shown that if the people of the Mother Country and of the Colonies only make up their minds that their unity shall last, " the idea will realize itself." I would venture to extend this expression to the mode of organization by which that unity is to be maintained, namely, Imperial Federation, and to say that if we accept the principle of that policy—to which Mr. Forster gave the powerful support of the last years of his invaluable life—"the idea will realize itself," when the people of the Empire have become sufficiently familiarized with it.

My desire in opening this discussion is, that we should bring our minds to the conclusion that the principle of the permanent unity of the Empire, having already proved itself of such vital force—in laying hold of the national feeling of all our British fellow-subjects —must become of much greater practical potency; that it must produce more solid cohesion, develop more effective organization, assume order, shape, embodiment. In other words, the sentiment of unity must evolve the practical principle of Imperial Federation, which "will realize itself," by this country and the Colonies, succeeding in producing such an effective Federal Government as will meet their joint requirements, and be in harmony with their views and institutions—a Government which will safeguard all their common interests, without interfering with their provincial affairs.

The stage which has now been reached in the progress of Imperial Federation can be best described, by an expression recently much quoted, as that of "inquiry and examination." It is surely not the least hopeful sign in the prospects of our policy that its advocates refuse, at this early stage of its discussion, to pledge themselves to details, or to any preference for one or other of the various forms of Federal Government, which at present exist or have existed in the world. If Imperial Federalists, instead of being practical men, were mere speculative theorists, one of the first things they would have done would have been to frame some elaborate, and probably fantastic, constitution, and to dogmatically prescribe it as the only possible form of

Federal Government. They are not likely to do any-thing of the kind. The Imperial Federation League has been wise in not putting forward any scheme, but in inviting the discussion of various schemes, so that the public mind of the Empire may be made up upon the question, by becoming familiar with the idea of Federal Government, and with the many forms which that Government may assume. No doubt the League has incurred the censure of some critics, for not having produced a fully developed plan. But it must be re-membered that the professional critic is a destructive being, who flourishes by pulling to pieces the sugges-tions and policies of men who are endowed with con-structive faculties. Withhold from him details, and you deprive him of much of the very food which is essential to his existence. It is possible to smother in its infancy a great principle by over-clothing it with details. No doubt, if it live and grow, it must sooner or later be provided with these, if it is to become a force of practical utility. It must, therefore, be only a question when, and by whom, a detailed scheme of Imperial Federation shall be authoritatively proposed. In the mean time, it would be bad advocacy of the question to divert the public mind from the formation of clear conceptions as to essential principles, by insist-ing upon the importance of details before those principles have been well considered and generally approved.

It will be for individuals and societies only, to suggest modes by which a practical Federal Constitu-tion can be given to the Empire. It will be for the Governments of the United Kingdom and of the self-governing Colonies to propose, to agree upon, and to establish such a constitution.

Before speaking of the essential principles of Imperial Federation, I should like to notice one objection raised by some friends of the Unity of the Empire, who meet every proposal for more efficient organization of our Imperial system, by asking what could be more satisfactory than the existing state of feeling between England and the Colonies.   They point to the splendid spirit which sent the New South Wales regiment to Suakim, and which caused the other Australian Colonies, as well as the Dominion of Canada, to offer troops for similar service.   No doubt a strong national Imperial feeling, which, as far as sentiment can go, leaves nothing to be desired, dictated these offers, and would lead to still more substantial assistance being rendered in the event of its being more urgently needed.   But if it were—if the safety or interests of the Empire were seriously jeopardized by war with any great Power or combinations of Powers—it would doubtless be a subject of regret that timely organization had not been combined with national sentiment, so that that motive power should wield machinery of defence of irresistible force for the protection of the Empire. Sentiment is one of the great mainsprings of human action ; it makes and maintains nations, but not without organization.   A nation is but a mob without organization.   The most numerous mob may be impelled by the strongest sentiment, but it is powerless the moment it has to face a mere handful of men so organized as to walk in step and to hold their rifles and bayonets at the same angle.   Sentiment by itself cannot save our unity, our Empire, from being shaken, shattered, or blown into space, by Powers which would be broken by the shock of coming into collision with the herculean strength, which would be produced by

the combination of our Imperial sentiment with
Imperial organization. Federation would save our
Empire in war, or, better still, from war. Those who
assert that nothing is needed beyond the admirable
Imperial spirit which so happily exists, remind me of
the patriotic but impractical man who declared that a
standing army was not required, " for," said he, " if an
enemy were to invade this country, the spirit of the
people is such that they would rise up as one man."
" Yes, and they would be knocked down as one man,"
was the reply of that practical statesman, Lord
Palmerston.

Objectors to Imperial Federation sometimes dispose
of the subject, to their own entire satisfaction, in a
single sentence to this effect—" I have never heard
a feasible scheme proposed, and do not believe it is
possible to frame one." Although it cannot be supposed
that those who make such observations, altogether
forget that there are several Federations at present in
the world, it is clear that they have never studied the
different varieties of Federal Government, and have
very hazy notions as to what it really is. The
existing systems are quite compatible with provincial
control of provincial concerns; and this would be more
so with a Federation of such an Empire as ours, in
which the distinction between general and local
questions would be so much more clearly defined by
the oceans, which, while separating our dominions,
form such splendid highways between them—highways
which only require, for the absolute safety of our
communications along them, an organized system of
Imperial defence.

What, then, are the essential principles of Imperial
Federation?

(1) In the language of the programme of the League—"Any scheme of Imperial Federation should combine on an equitable basis the resources of the Empire for the maintenance of common interests, and adequately provide for an organized defence of common rights."

(2) Combination "on an equitable basis" implies that all those who combine shall have a voice in the Government whereby the "common interests" shall be maintained; and this can only be given to Canada, Australasia, South Africa, and the West Indies, by extending to them equitable representation in a Parliament of the Empire.

I leave out India from the list, because the idea of bringing representatives from that country to London, or even of admitting them to any elected Indian legislatures, has never been seriously proposed; and it would be unwise to complicate the consideration of the question of the representation of the whole of our British fellow-subjects—of the race which has created Parliamentary institutions in the world—with the question of giving representation to an Oriental people, whose ideas, history, traditions, and modes of government so essentially differ from those of Europe in general, and of England in particular. The possibility or impossibility of making India a member of our Imperial Federation ought not for one moment to retard the Federal union of our British fellow-countrymen in these isles and beyond the seas. India, governed as a dependency by an Imperial Federal Parliament and Executive, would be in as good a position as she is at present under the control of the existing Imperial Parliament. If India is to be held in the future, it must be by the federated power of the Empire, not merely by the strength of these distant isles.

An "equitable basis" of representation could not be fixed with mathematical accuracy as regards population, wealth, and extent of territory, although it might be approximately adjusted. To prevent some Colonies from feeling that they were left out of our Imperial system, representation might have to be given to them, though they would not be entitled to it according to the scale adopted with regard to the larger dominions. It might be so in the case of Mauritius, Malta, Natal, and one or two of the West India Islands, if they could not be satisfactorily included in groups. The distribution of representation would require careful consideration, but it could doubtless be adjusted so as to satisfy the fair claims of all the people of the Empire. The franchise need not be uniform.

(3) Representation having been arranged "on an equitable basis," there would be less difficulty in dealing with the question of Imperial taxation. Taxation and representation go together. The representatives of the Empire would be powerless when they assembled unless the Imperial Parliament could command the "sinews of war," by being able to raise a sufficient revenue to maintain the defences of the Empire and to defray the expenses of its common government. There could be no practical or sentimental grievance in a Parliament, in which the whole Empire was fairly ·represented, directly imposing taxes throughout all its Dominions. Taxation should of course be adjusted so that its burden should be equally borne. The Federal Constitution might even specify certain sources of revenue to be, either

o

wholly or partially, reserved for taxation by the
Parliament of the Empire. A very few items would
be quite sufficient for the purpose, and everything else
could be left to be taxed by the provincial Parliaments.
These need suffer no curtailment of their powers,
except in so far as certain rights of general taxation
might be reserved to the Parliament of the Empire.
Suppose, for example, tobacco, wines, and spirits were
thus set apart, they alone would yield a very large
Imperial revenue. An income-tax, not to exceed 3*d.*
in the pound, would also bring in considerable sums
from all quarters of the Empire. It can be easily seen
that if it were desirable to limit the taxing powers of
the Federal Parliament, ample margin could be given
it to enable it to raise, even from a very few items,
sufficient revenue for purposes of peace or war.[1]

(4) The last, but not least, essential principle—which
is perfectly compatible with an efficient system of
Federation, and without which it would be impossible
to work its machinery of government—is that the
self-governing Colonies should retain complete control
of all their provincial affairs. Every clear-sighted
Imperial Federalist always keeps this steadily in view.
All our Dominions and Colonies should be secured in
the rights which they now enjoy, of regulating
their own fiscal systems upon such politico-economical
principles as they, rightly or wrongly, consider to be
most sound and suitable to their own interests. A
Federal Government ought not, and would not, even
if not prevented by any Constitutional restriction,
attempt to force Protection upon this country, the
most Free Trade portion of the Empire, or Free Trade
upon Victoria, the most Protectionist. Federation

[1] See page 201.

could, just as easily as our present Imperial system,
be worked without uniformity of tariffs. It must
also be borne in mind that, with the diversity in the
circumstances of the old and of the new territories
of the Empire, it is quite possible that one fiscal
system may be most suitable to one community,
and the opposite system to another, unless, out of the
complicated conditions and ramifications of commerce,
conclusions of universal application can be evolved
with absolute mathematical certainty. There are
people who value Imperial Federation by the trade
advantages which they expect to see flowing directly
from it. Whatever the policy may eventually lead to,
it is not likely at first to cause the removal of existing
trade restrictions. If, however, it should never do so,
it will give, both in peace and war, a security to the
commerce of the whole Empire immeasurably greater
than can otherwise be extended to it; and that would
be a more valuable gain than the removal of existing
trade restrictions.

Time will not permit me to consider whether
Imperial Federation should be preceded by any of
those councils of advice which are sometimes recommended, but which, at least, could be only temporary
expedients. The growth of the Empire is rapidly
unfolding the practical question, how we shall have to
provide ourselves with as complete a legislative and
executive organization as any of the great Federal
States possess, if efficient organization we are ever
to have. That means an Imperial Parliament and
Ministry. This is the principle which, if accepted,
will, in the words of Mr. Forster, "realize itself."
It is not at present profitable to dwell upon details,
though we may well glance at them and turn over in

our minds alternative schemes; for, fortunately, we
are not bound to only one. Imperial Federalists have
clearer ideas on the question than may be often
supposed, for they wisely abstain from dogmatically
prescribing any particular Constitution. We have
already complete systems of provincial self-government
—the marvellous growth of a very few years. All we
want is a really Imperial government. One way in
which this could be obtained would be by the present
Imperial Parliament making itself so in reality, as
well as in name, by exclusively devoting itself to the
affairs of the Empire. To do this it would have to
hand over the provincial concerns of the United
Kingdom to a Parliament of the British Isles. One
legislature would be sufficient for the transaction of
all provincial business. I touch not the burning
question of separate local government, or of Home
Rule, in these isles, for it is no part of our question
of Imperial Federation; it is for the British people
within these seas, and for them alone, to settle
their own domestic affairs. If the present British
Parliament were to effect a desirable division of labour
by divesting itself of provincial concerns, and by
devoting itself to Imperial affairs, it need not retain
so many members in the House of Commons, and a due
proportion of the reduced number would have to be
Colonial representatives. Whether there should be
an Imperial Upper Chamber would be a question more
of convenience than of principle, for the control of
land systems and the regulation of the laws of
private property would be vested in the provincial
Parliaments. To the House of Lords, even if all the
English peers were to be members of an Upper House
of the Empire, as well as of that of the United

Kingdom, Colonial statesmen could be admitted as life peers.

I am not proposing a plan, but, by way of illustration, I am showing that we can conceive of many ways in which Imperial Federation can be carried out, and that some of these ways may be quite upon the lines of, may be merely expansions of, existing institutions. The principle once accepted, the details can be worked out, and we shall not fail to secure for our Empire all the advantages which our German connections, our American cousins, and our Canadian brothers have secured for themselves, from the adoption of the only system of government adapted to their circumstances and wide-spread territories, and *à fortiori* to those of the Empire of Great Britain.

Briefly to recapitulate the essential principles of Imperial Federation, which must be embodied in any form of Constitution :—

1. Equitable combination for maintenance of common interests and defence of common rights.

2. Equitable representation in an efficient Imperial Parliament.

3. Equitable system of taxation to raise Imperial revenue.

4. Equitable guarantee of all existing rights of provincial self-government, including control of fiscal policies.

Any paper on this subject must be incomplete. Time would not permit us to go the whole round of this great question. We cannot in a day take in all the beauties and wonders of this great Exhibition of the Empire, much less can we realize the possibilities, or rather the certainties, as far as anything human may be said to be certain, of future Imperial develop-

ment and greatness of which this Exhibition, splendid
as it is, is merely the earnest and forerunner. Neither
can we in our contemplation, in our consideration of
this great policy, grasp it in all its bearings, and
picture to ourselves the grand certainties of peace,
power, security, and happiness to all the dominions
and lands of our Empire, to the greatest as well as the
least of them, involved in the realization of Imperial
Federation.

I have been reluctantly obliged to pass many points
without notice at which I should like to linger.
There is one which I must just mention—our common
interests.[1] We are sometimes told that there are not
sufficient of these to require common organization,
much less Imperial Federation. Not many interests
common to the British Isles, Canada, Australasia,
South Africa, and the West Indies! Unless I am in
a dream or under a delusion, I see our common
interests in north, in south, in east, and west; in the
Old World, in the New; in every clime, round every
coast, in every sea. In all the great ocean highways
they preponderate over those of all other nations.
We have in the preservation of these highways, for
the uninterrupted communication of our people with
each other, and the undisturbed flow of our commerce,
one great, one sufficient reason, if there were no
others, for Federal organization. We have the highest
common interest in the maintenance of peace, in the
secure development of the internal prosperity of all
our dominions and territories. The only sure guarantee we can have for these, and all our other common
interests, is in our united organized strength. If any
one present doubts whether our common interests

[1] Pages 130, 182, 237.

are numerous or great enough to require to be safeguarded on sea and land by our federated power, let
him look around him in this place! Let him take
another walk through this Exhibition, and if he does
not return, before the close of the discussion, to avow
himself convinced, he must be hopelessly proof against
every argument.

Many great Empires have existed in the past.
Their ruins may be seen thickly scattered over the
old continents of Europe, Asia, and Africa. They
were all raised by the sword and perished by the
sword. Great powers exist at the present day, but,
with two exceptions, their very existence depends
upon military strength. Not so with the United
States and the Empire of Great Britain. Both rest
upon the solid basis of the peaceful victories of our
British race. Imperial Federation will consolidate,
organize, crown, the greatest colonizing achievements
the world has ever seen or can ever see. It will be
the noblest union of free men, of self-governing communities, who, by their own free will, will bind themselves in one indissoluble, world-wide nationality,
under one flag, under one sceptre, in order that they
may enjoy the greatest blessings of security, power,
and peace.

In the discussion which followed, the late Sir
Alexander Stuart, who had recently been Premier of
New South Wales, said: " Mr. Labilliere lays down as
one of the essential conditions ' an equitable system of
taxation to raise an Imperial revenue.' I am afraid
that is just one of those stumbling-blocks which must,
if enlarged upon, cast back for a long period that
which we all so much desire. He has enumerated
certain articles which must be made the subject of

taxation by this Imperial Parliament. So far so good.
They are the articles which are fairly distributed
among consumers of the British race. But I cannot
help remarking that there is nothing upon which our
fellow-Colonists are so touchy, I may say, as any
interference with their fiscal arrangements. Freedom
in this respect is an essential part of our constitution.
. . . It is, after all, one of the essential points of
British freedom that a community like ours shall be
entitled to tax themselves and to dispose of the taxation as they choose, and, once having obtained that
right, I do not think the Colonists are at all likely to
listen to any proposal that involved their parting with
any portion of it. I am quite aware, of course, that
if there is to be an Imperial Parliament or a Federal
Council, all parts of the Empire must join in defraying
the expense. . . . Let the expenditure, whatever it
be, be fixed on some equitable principle . . . and then
let each Colony understand that . . . it must bear a
certain proportion of the cost, and let it do this in
its own way . . . We do not wish to see England
bear the expense of that which is for our good, and
we are therefore quite prepared to pay the additional
expense. . . . We say we will find the money. It is
no matter to you how we find it."

To this I replied : "The system suggested by Sir
Alexander Stuart—namely, that the Provincial Parliaments should impose all taxes, and hand over to the
Imperial Exchequer the proportion of revenue to be
contributed by their respective Provinces—was one way
of arranging the details. But, as a thorough-going
Imperial Federalist, I do not shrink from the principle
that, if equitable representation were given to all
portions of the Empire, the Imperial Parliament might

be entrusted with powers of general taxation. The powers of Federal taxation which I advocate are only those possessed by all the existing Federal Parliaments. But what has been suggested by Sir Alexander Stuart would answer the purpose, if more acceptable to the people of the Empire."

The objection to giving the Imperial Federal Parliament powers of taxation is purely sentimental; and no doubt, if such a legislature were established without them, they would soon be granted, as the confidence of the Empire in it grew, as it would. Imperial taxation, practically, would not be felt, for with the growing wealth and population of the Empire, it would become really infinitesimal. A very little calculation will prove this. Sir Alexander Galt once estimated that a penny a ton levied on all ships entering the ports of the Empire would yield several millions. Mr. Thomas Macfarlane, of Ottawa, has shown that 5 or 10 per cent. customs duties, raised throughout the Empire, would produce a large revenue.

This suggestion corresponds with the proposal made, in the Colonial Conference of 1887, by Mr. Hofmeyr, leader of the Dutch party in the Cape Colony, whose efforts and sympathies for the unity of Empire must be highly appreciated. In a very able speech,[1] he introduced the subject of "The feasibility of promoting a closer union between the various parts of the British Empire by means of an Imperial Tariff of Customs, to be levied independently of the duties payable under existing tariffs, on goods entering the Empire from abroad, the revenue derived from such tariff to be devoted to the general defence of the

[1] Report of *Proceedings of the Conference*, page 463.

Empire." The pith of the proposal is contained in this passage from the speech :—"Now, supposing that we were to levy an average rate of two per cent. all round (the tariff might be arranged so that one class of goods should pay more than another), that £352,000,000 representing the foreign imports of the Empire, would give a revenue of not less than £7,000,000. That is a revenue which would pay for a very considerable part of the British Fleet. It would relieve the Colonies from the payment of subsidies, and at the same time that it would be paid by the Colonies it would be paid by Great Britain too."

What more fitting than that £7,000,000, in whatever manner to be raised from the entire Empire, should be annually expended upon the construction of war-ships, which are absolutely essential to maintain that naval supremacy without which our unity—our Empire—would be at an end, and the coasts and commerce of its several dominions exposed to any foe who might prove superior to us upon the ocean. The *Times*, in one of its articles on "The Strength of the Navy," at the end of 1893, estimated that at least £5,500,000, for naval construction, will in future be annually required to keep us equal to France and Russia.

Mr. Hofmeyr does not favour subsidies, to which Sir Alexander Stuart clearly pointed ; and the plan of the former shows that there are ways of raising Imperial revenue without interfering with Colonial fiscal arrangements, as the latter seemed to fear. In an earlier part of his speech, Mr. Hofmeyr said, "I doubt very much whether you would find that a system of subsidies would answer in the long run.

You would, in that case, find very soon that the principle of representation would be asserted by the Colonies. The system of subsidies, if developed to any extent, would practically amount to a tax, and where you have a tax, the people who bear the tax sooner or later ask to be represented. In other words, you might find a system of political federation brought to the fore." This he rather fears, not because he is not in sympathy with the idea, but because he evidently does not wish immediately to face its difficulties, which he appears to over-estimate. But if subsidies would be a tax leading to federation, surely what Mr. Hofmeyr proposes would be similar in nature and results. "All roads lead to Rome." The more the question is thought out, the less serious seem the difficulties of satisfactorily arranging, in more ways than one, the mode of providing a revenue for the Empire. We shall see at page 235 the respective proportions of revenue at present provided by England and the Colonies, for the defence of their joint commerce. Harm may be, and has been, done by want of tact and by persistence in pressing this consideration. Given fair representation in the Councils of the Empire, to all its British populations, and there will be little fear of any of them being backward in contributing to its support.

CHAPTER XI.

LATER OBJECTIONS OF MR. GOLDWIN SMITH.

Objections in " Canada and the Canadian Question "—Overpower-
ing opponents with numerous interrogations—Answered argu-
ments repeated—Objection to use of word " Empire" like
Professor Freeman's to words " Imperial " and " Federal "—
Might equally object to " Military "—Great Britain " a
Canton of Greater Britain "—Mr. Forster's answer—" Natural
Combinations "—" Legislative clamps "—" Thoughts of ordinary citizen " beyond his own circle—Federal Government
and British Monarchy—" Novelty in political architecture"
—Federation between federations and non-federal States—
" Whose diplomacy is to prevail ? "—Federation under pres-
sure—French Canadians—Professor Freeman and the good
will of the United States—Federation of English-speaking
race—" Voluntary retirement of England "—Practical surrender of Mr. Goldwin Smith—His article on " Continental
Union "—Annexation and Independence for Canadians,
French and British, after twenty years' advocacy by Mr.
Smith—*Delenda est Carthago !*

NOTWITHSTANDING his unfulfilled predictions, unrealized
expectations, refuted arguments, and diminished
number of adherents, Mr. Goldwin Smith bravely
struggles on, the standard-bearer of a forlorn hope,
against the cause of Imperial unity. He has, undoubtedly, earned some of the admiration due to a
captain who nails his colours to the mast, resolved that
his sinking ship shall fight as long as a charge of
powder can be kept dry.   Having dealt with the
earlier arguments of this most able and persistent of
the opponents of the Federation, and advocates of the

disruption of the Empire, it would be a serious omission from this book were no notice taken of some of his most recent contentions. In his work on "Canada and the Canadian Question," [1] he repeats most of the objections which he had previously urged, and which have been already answered, against Imperial Federation; and, again unsuccessfully, endeavours to drown the policy in a torrent of interrogatories, all of which have been previously disposed of, or are capable of being easily dealt with. It is bad argument, but often most effective controversial strategy, to heap upon opponents numerous questions, to which answers can only be given at much greater length, than the few sentences in which such weak and querulous objections may be raised.

One opening point with Mr. Goldwin Smith, in dealing with Imperial Federation, has been disposed of before at page 165, but a new and conclusive answer has just been given to it. Mr. Smith says, "The Imperial Federationists refuse to tell us their plan." Therefore, such is obviously his logic, Imperial Federation is impossible. It might have been said with equal force, before the meeting of the Canadian Convention of 1864, and the Australian Convention of 1891, "Canadian and Australian Federationists refuse to tell us their plan." But the accredited delegates in both instances were not long in producing one, as an Imperial Federal Convention would doubtless do if empowered by the Governments of the Empire.

The same answered questions about the Indies, East and West, are again repeated, the same objections about defences, tariffs, free trade and protection, are again marched out. The superiority of the old Roman

---

[1] Published in 1891.

over the modern British Empire is commended. The former " was an Empire in the proper sense of the term. . . . The name applies to India, but to nothing else connected with Great Britain, unless it be the fortresses and Crown Colonies. Our self-governed Colonies are not members of an Empire, but free communities virtually independent of the Mother Country, which for the purpose of Confederation would be called upon to resign a portion of their independence."

Here Mr. Goldwin Smith seems rather to re-echo the objections of Professor Freeman,[1] who says, " What is ' Imperial' cannot be ' Federal,' and what is ' Federal' cannot be ' Imperial ; ' " and " that the phrase, ' Imperial Federation,' is a contradiction in terms." The article is, as might be expected, very learned, treating of the subject from the academic, not from the practical standpoint, the arguments being technical and etymological. Mr. Freeman remarks, " I cannot help saying that clearness of thought would have greatly gained if the word ' Empire' had always been sternly confined to what was its strict meaning for ages. It would have been well if the name had never been applied to anything but the Roman Empire, and those powers which professed to continue the Roman Empire." It may be a cause of academic, though not of practical regret, that the word " Military " has ever been applied to any soldiers but the old Roman Legions. Rightly or wrongly, we have the words " Empire" and " Imperial" used in speaking of the dominions of modern Britain ; and until our etymologists can supply us with better, which they have

[1] In an article on Imperial Federation, in *Macmillan's Magazine,* April, 1885; also in *Britannic Confederation,* 1892.

not yet suggested, practical Federalists must make the best of what they have.

It will be a slight digression here to notice the highly technical objection taken by Professor Freeman to Imperial Federation, on the ground that there is no precedent for it, such unions always having been entered into between States in positions of equality; and that, as the Colonies are in subordination to the Mother Country, it would be too great a condescension on her part to take them into federal union. " Such a demand," exclaims the historian—whose recent death has been a great national loss—" was never yet made on any ruling people or any ruling assembly. . . . The soberest of us will be driven to turn Jingoes, and sing 'Rule, Britannia,' if we are asked that Great Britain shall sink to become one Canton, or three Cantons of Greater Britain." She would, on the contrary, rise in fame and power, as the parent and principal state of her federated Empire, as Prussia has risen to a grander position since she has been merged in federal Germany ; or if, with Britannic Federation, the worst came to the worst for England, better far for her to be a Canton, a minor State in such an Empire as hers will become, than a Holland, deprived of her naval supremacy, dwarfed and isolated among the great Powers of the future. But, to Professor Freeman's idea that the United Kingdom should monopolize all the honours and responsibilities of directing the foreign and common concerns of the Empire, Mr. Forster gave this conclusive answer, at the time, in speaking at an Imperial Federation meeting at Cambridge: "Talk about Jingoism! there was the Jingo feeling in its fullest development, not directed against the Frenchman, or the Russian, or even the German, but against our own kith and kin."

But to return to Mr. Smith, who proceeds—" The Achæan League, the Swiss Band, the Union of the Netherlands, the American Union, all were perfectly natural combinations; . . . but " fasten the people of the British Islands, those of the self-governed Colonies, the Hindoo, the African, and the Kaffir together with what legislative clamps you will, you cannot produce the unity of political character and sentiment which is essential to community of councils, much more to national union." Who has ever suggested the fastening of Hindoos, Africans, and Kaffirs to our British race, except Mr. Goldwin Smith or some other enemy of its federation and unity? Certainly any one who understands British Federalism would not consider Mr. Smith's "legislative clamps" essential, but mischievous.

The objection is pressed, that " the thoughts of the ordinary citizen " are not carried " beyond the circle of his own life and work." But he must be singularly unintelligent, if he cannot be got to perceive that that life and work must be rendered infinitely more secure and peaceful, by having the protection and strength of a great united and federated Empire thrown around them, than by having the various dominions of that Empire broken off into several separate and weaker States. If this be so, it must be exactly the reverse of the fact that—" Imperial Federation, to the mass of the people comprised in it, would be a mere name conveying with it no definite sense of benefit, on which anything could be built." About the time Mr. Smith wrote this, I had striking proof how " the thoughts of the ordinary citizen " may be beneficially " carried beyond the circle of his own life and work." As I was returning from lecturing in a country town on Imperial Federation, a man of the farmer class spoke to me in the train, saying that, although he had not been to hear me, he had some ideas on the subject. I was interested in listening to them, and delighted to find how an "ordinary citizen" could get such a good grasp of the policy, in which he avowed himself a firm believer. I was particularly impressed with a remark he made, about its being good for people to have the affairs of the Empire to think of, besides their immediate local and provincial concerns; and I felt more than ever convinced that not the least valuable effect of British Federation would be educational—in enlarging the ideas, sympathies, and intelligence of our people in all quarters of the Empire.

On "the relation of the Federal Government to the British monarchy" several questions are put, which a schoolboy with any knowledge of the German and Austrian Empires might easily answer; the first being, " Would the same Queen be sovereign of both?" the Federal Government and the British monarchy. Questions as to the appointment of "the heads of all the other members of the Federation," the constitution of the Supreme Court, the "refusal to send the war contingent," and the apportionment of representation are asked; and the serious observation is made that "If Great Britain had members in proportion to St. Helena and Fiji, the Parliament would have to meet on Salisbury Plain."

Mr. Goldwin Smith theorizes about the Parliament of Great Britain "ceasing to be a Sovereign Power," and asserts that "the same person could not be head at once of a Federation and of one of the communities included in it. . . . Her Majesty would have to choose

P

between the British and the Pan-Britannic crown."
But why—seeing that the heads of the German and
Austrian federations have not been obliged to do
anything of the kind—not a glimmer of light is given
to show us.

We are next told that we should have "a striking
novelty in political architecture in the shape of a
Confederation of Confederations." It would, doubtless,
be the greatest of them; but would no more differ
from those which at present exist than they do from
each other. It would have its own distinctive features
to suit the circumstances of our Empire.

Then it is said, no doubt with perfect accuracy,
that some Colonies, like New Zealand, "would not
join any Federation;" so that "the members of the
Central Parliament would represent partly Federations,
partly single communities." Why, if need be, should
we not have it so, unless our minds are so morbidly
logical, as to be unable to endure anything politically
unsymmetrical, however practical? Then we are
warned by the example of the Canadian Provinces
which at first hold aloof from the Dominion. But
they soon came in—as portions of the Empire, which
probably would at first refuse to enter into Imperial
Federation, would do after its partial establishment.

"The Federation would be nothing if not diplomatic. But whose diplomacy is to prevail?" Here
is the attempt again made to show that we have no
common interests; whereas it has been shown over
and over again, in this volume and elsewhere, that
all our greatest interests are common or Imperial
interests, although there may be many smaller ones
which are only Provincial.

Mr. Goldwin Smith contends that we can only federate

"under the pressure of necessity." Sooner or later, if we do not federate before, a common danger may supply the pressure; but should we not be wiser to avoid the danger, possibly a great war, by the organized strength of Federation? One day, when war seemed inevitable, on account of the Afghan frontier question, a well-known Australian whom I met, exclaimed, "So the Czar is going to federate our Empire," or "to bring about Imperial Federation."

We are told that to the French Canadians "anything that would bind their country closer to Great Britain is odious." Mr. Smith wants them to form one or two among about sixty States of the American Union. This would be utter extinction. They are not so blind as not to see, that they would hold a much more important position in a Dominion of Canada federated with the British Empire.

Then it is affirmed that "to make peace on earth is to promote the coming not of an exclusive military league" (ours would be naval), "but of the Parliament of Man, the moral Parliament of Man. . . . There is a Federation which is feasible . . . the moral federation of the whole English-speaking race throughout the world," including the United States. This is as yet too vast and visionary for practical Imperial Federalists. We only propose to go by steps, the first feasible one being the federation of our Empire. But Mr. Smith tells how his grander scheme is to be achieved. "Nothing is needed to bring this about but the voluntary retirement of England as a political power from a shadowy dominion in a sphere which is not hers." Yes, the contraction, or extinction, of England!—the dream of the philosopher's life, and the certain result of his policy, if adopted.

After starting certain imaginary difficulties, about sending representatives from the Colonies to this country, Mr. Goldwin Smith concludes—" Let it be taken as certain and irreversible that the Colonies will not part with any portion of their self-government. If a scheme can be devised by which they can be governed by an Assembly at Westminster without any loss to them of self-government, it may, supposing it to be presented to them in an intelligible and practicable form, stand a chance of consideration at their hands."

Thus, after all his questions and objections, Mr. Smith practically surrenders to the Imperial Federalists; for he admits that their policy may be accepted, if it does not involve—as it has been proved to demonstration, that it will not involve—loss to the Colonies of their self-government.

Since the previous part of this chapter was written, Mr. Goldwin Smith has produced an article, in which he labours to prove that " Continental Union,"[1]—or, to put it more plainly and less invitingly, annexation and extinction by the United States—is the true policy for Canada. British Federalists have, however, to thank him for another important admission, when he says that " The elasticity of the federal system renders it capable of indefinite extension so long as geographical unity is maintained." It having been proved, over and over again,[2] and admitted even by unbelievers in our federation, that geographical continuity on the same mainland is not essential, we may take the first and greater portion of the sentence as a valuable

[1] See article so entitled in the *North American Review* for August, 1893.
[2] See pages 52, 160, 191.

testimony to our policy. There are only two mis-
conceptions in regard to that policy which need here
be noticed, Mr. Smith's objections having been already
so fully dealt with. It is most incorrectly stated that
" Free Trade between the Colonies and Great Britain
is an essential part of the Federationist idea," and it
is implied that our policy means that "a power
antagonistic to the American Republic shall be formed
to the north of it."

Professor Freeman has urged, in the article already
referred to, that the lasting good will of the United
States is more likely to be secured by the independence
of the Colonies—in other words, by our British people
dividing and weakening themselves, so that the
Americans may become the all-powerful and pre-
ponderating Anglo-Saxon nation of the future. It
cannot be too often repeated that British Federalists
want the United Empire to occupy a position, not of
hostile, but of the most friendly, equality with the
United States.[1] It is no mere stretch of imagination
to suppose that in a future not remote, the two great
kindred naval powers might prescribe that there
shall be no more war on the seas, which, outside the
three-mile limit, should be neutral to all nations.
They would be strong enough to maintain a sufficient
maritime police for the purpose of keeping the peace.

It is unnecessary in this work to deal with "Continental Union" at any length. The Canadians, to
whom its arguments are addressed, know how to
appreciate them, as Mr. Smith admits, when he says,
" That a Continental Unionist cannot hope to be
elected to Parliament is true only in this sense, that
the nominations in Canada, as in the United States,

[1] See pages 43, 47, 145, 185.

are made by the party conventions, and neither of the Canadian parties has yet declared for Continental Union." And this, notwithstanding the advocacy of the greatest champion of Imperial disruption! He says, "During a residence of more than twenty years in Canada, I have seldom met with a Canadian who, if he had thought at all freely on these matters, did not in private avow or betray his conviction that a change must some day come." This is a starting axiom in the federal proposition.

We have just heard what little way, Mr. Smith confesses, annexation has made with Canadian politicians, though he tries to make out it is in considerable favour among the people. Let us see what he has to say about Canadian independence. "To independence, I must confess, I was myself at one time inclined.... But the movement found little support, and though it is now being revived in opposition to Continental Union, it seems not to have much strength in itself." We have thus, by Mr. Goldwin Smith's process of elimination, got rid in Canada of independence and annexation—except in the most cherished wishes and thoughts of the philosopher, who has been so long chasing the Will o' the Wisp of British disintegration. What then remains, seeing that things cannot always continue as they are, but Imperial Federation? Thirty years ago Mr. Smith preached in England the breaking up of the Empire, only to rouse the spirit of the nation in favour of its permanent unity; and that feeling has culminated in the widespread and growing acceptance of the federal principle. After more than twenty years' advocacy in Canada, he seems, on his own showing, to have there achieved similar results. What was said of Stuarts and Bourbons may be said of him as regards this question—He seems "to have learned nothing and to have forgotten nothing." As to annexation and independence, he tells us that neither political party has been induced to touch them, whilst we have had numbers of politicians, on different sides, including some of the most eminent statesmen of the Dominion, espousing the cause of British Federalism.

As it is elsewhere pointed out,[1] annexation is not likely to commend itself to French Canadians, any more than to those of the British race; and Mr. Goldwin Smith's observations are not calculated to render it more acceptable.

In one place he says, "By the French Canadians tenacious of their separate nationality, the name of Imperial Federation is abhorred;" and further on we find, "Though the forces of Canada are inadequate to the assimilation of the French, by the forces of the United Continent they would probably be assimilated, for all essential purposes, not less easily than the French in Louisiana." Never was net more visibly spread in sight of birds, than in this attempt to ensnare the French Canadians into annexation. If they abhor Federation, for the reason assigned, *à fortiori* they must abhor annexation, as the thing most of all to be avoided if they want to preserve their individuality. Next, they should oppose independence, as only a halt on the way to annexation. The only alternative for them, therefore, is Imperial Federation, even if they regard it as the least of evils; for in it alone can they hope for escape from being completely swamped and obliterated, which is the simple meaning of Mr. Smith's "assimilation." Although their British fellow-

[1] Pages 211, 241.

Canadians would not, in so many respects, be affected by annexation, they would lose much by it—" if there were anything special to be conserved in Canada," by the continued existence of the Dominion, which is denied by implication.

For British and French Canadians, alike, independence means insignificance beside, then absorption by the United States, and finally total obliteration. Instead of Canada holding her head high, as a great Dominion of the Empire of Great Britain, her very name would be wiped out of the map of the world; her present Provinces would be lost in the crowd of States of the American Republic. But a modern Cato proclaims, with iteration, that Britain as an Empire, and Canada as a Dominion, must be blotted out—*Delenda est Carthago !*

CHAPTER XII.

FRAMING A FEDERAL CONSTITUTION.

Experience in initiating Federal Unions—Conferences and Conventions for purpose—Initiative in summoning them with Governments, also of formulating detailed plans for their consideration—Mr. Justice Holroyd's view—Imperial Federation League framing schemes—Its deputation to Lord Salisbury—. Reasons for leaving Governments to formulate plans—League's Report—Deputation to Mr. Gladstone—Dissolution of League —Example of Conference of 1887—Federation question excluded from its consideration—Object-lesson it gave—Conferences: to arrange bases of Federation—for special purposes—to meet periodically—Examples furnished by Canadian and Australian Federation Conventions—Who should first propose Federation?—An Imperial Conference and Convention—Crown Colonies—Bases of Federal scheme to be laid down by Conference—Convention to frame Constitution from it—Ratification by Parliaments.

THERE is as practical an answer to the inquiry how our Federation is to be brought about, as to the question of the form it should assume. As to both, we must go upon the lines of the experience which the history of the system of government affords, rather than upon any fresh theoretical suggestions. The features of our union, though doubtless striking in their individuality, will bear a strong likeness to the whole Federal family, with more close resemblance to one member than to others. It is only on the meeting of a Conference of the Governments—pledged to the essential principles of Federation, but free to work out the details—that we shall be able to form any idea of what model will be taken from which to shape our Constitution. The steps and circumstances leading to our adoption of the system will also in many respects, doubtless, correspond with the evolution of existing federal unions. We should, however, above all things, seek to avoid having the history of that of Germany repeated with regard to ours—that a great war, however glorious for our Empire, should be the means of hastening its Federation. Were it to be so, there would be universal regret among all our people, that they had not, by previous union, organized their strength for the war, and probably thereby have averted its outbreak.

It is most likely and desirable that the Federation of our Empire will be approached, by means of preliminary Conferences of the Governments, as was that of Canada when undertaken and carried through, and as that of Australia has been, already with partial success—ultimately no doubt to be fully realized. When public opinion throughout the Empire has become sufficiently ripe for Federation, our people will not wait for, or even look to, private individuals or societies to formulate schemes, but will expect their Governments to work out for them a practical Constitution, by means of Conferences and Conventions. One among many objections to any plan being prepared, at least unofficially, for the meetings of such bodies would be that until the members of the first preliminary Conference compared views on the subject, it would be uncertain whether an elementary Confederation, or a more complete Federation, would be more acceptable to the Governments; so that on whichever model the scheme might be framed, it

might not be that which the official delegates desired.
Mr. Justice Holroyd, President of the Imperial Federation League in Victoria, at one of its meetings in
Melbourne, in September, 1893, very clearly viewed
the position — " Statesmen — representatives of the
people to be federated—must settle the federal Constitution ; and Federationists did not seek to put themselves in the place of Statesmen, but to constitute
themselves a force behind them."

The Imperial Federation League wisely started
without adopting or formulating any plan. If, however—departing from the original idea of its founders
and from the lines upon which, in Canada and, so far,
in Australia, federal institutions have been successfully evolved—it had framed a detailed scheme of
federation, it would have entered upon dangerous
ground. It is not for individuals, however influential
personally or as an organization, to draw up a constitution, and, in effect to say, " This is what we *propose*
to the Empire." They may, however, render invaluable service by expounding the essential principles of
federation, by suggesting different forms in which it
can be adopted, and by instructing the people of the
Empire as to the history and working of existing
federal systems ; but, it cannot be too constantly
remarked, that to *propose* a plan is for those delegated
to do so by the responsible Governments of this
country and of the Colonies, and for them only. The
drawing up of a federal scheme, even by the Governments concerned, was not a condition precedent to the
meeting of the conferences, of official delegates who
framed the Canadian federal constitution, or of those
which have recently been at work with a similar
object in Australia. The League did much, and, had

it continued to exist, might have done more, to ripen the question for practical adoption by the statesmen and Parliaments of the Empire; but to father any particular scheme would have been outside its proper functions, and would certainly have impaired its usefulness.

The League seems to have been rather drawn in this direction by the reply of the then Prime Minister to the deputation which, in June, 1891, asked him to convene another Colonial Conference. Lord Salisbury suggested that delegates should not be invited from the Colony "unless we are prepared to lay before them for discussion some definite scheme." But herein is the danger of going further than submitting as a basis certain broad essential principles. Any scheme proposed may not commend itself to the Prime Minister of the day, and he may refuse to summon a conference to consider it, or, should he approve of it, some of the Colonies may decline to entertain it. Then what would the League have done? Gone on framing schemes, till it should hit upon one which would draw the Governments together in a conference? There is also this disadvantage in submitting a cut-and-dried detailed system of federal organization to delegates from the Colonies. It would prevent them from taking that part, which it is desirable they should have, in the foundation work of the mighty structure of a federated Great Britain. All the sons of the Empire should have a share in the honour of initiating and achieving this great undertaking. By provoking criticism of the details of a single plan the League would assuredly have compromised itself; by standing upon its first principles, as well as upon the ground of precedent and experience, it could have declined to take

upon itself one of the functions of the Governments—
the proposal of an Imperial Federal Constitution ; and
no one would have more highly appreciated such a
position than a statesman like Lord Salisbury, had it
been taken up and explained to him by the deputation
from the League.

The League, however, submitted to a special committee of eleven, only three of whom had been
Colonists, the task of forming a scheme; and after
more than a year's deliberation a report was published,
which contains some valuable original suggestions, in
addition to many which had been previously made.
Although the report, which was adopted at a meeting
on November 16, 1892, is throughout its course skil-
fully steered clear of details, and of prescribing as
essential principles of federation things that are not,
it grazes rather seriously against one of these rocks, in
proclaiming Intercolonial Federation a condition precedent to Imperial Federation. The words are, under
the head of " Mode of Colonial Representation " :—

" When the provinces of Australasia and South Africa are
each united under one Government, as Canada now is, and
those three dominions are represented in London by a member
of each Government respectively, such representatives should
be available for consultation with the Cabinet when matters of
foreign policy affecting the Colonies are under consideration."

But this would carry us scarcely a step beyond where
we are at present, for the Agents-General are now
available to be consulted as suggested ; and the delay
of years, proposed in the recommendation, is just what
any Minister would take his stand upon were he disposed to shelve the question. The report proceeds to
define how the United Kingdom, and " the three groups
of self-governing Colonies," are to be represented in a

Council to deal with Imperial defence. Intercolonial Federation in Australia and South Africa is a question for the people of these portions of the Empire to decide for themselves, and no one else should prescribe that policy to them; and although we may be morally certain that the Australians will federate among themselves within a very short time, it is surely imprudent to declare that their doing so is essential to Imperial Federation, especially as it does not follow that, if for any reason they should prefer to remain as they are, their organized federal union with the rest of the Empire is out of the question. Then to say that Imperial federal organization must wait till Intercolonial Federation is carried out in South Africa is to declare that the former policy, even in the elementary form in which the report of the League suggests it, cannot be initiated for probably a quarter of a century—a long time for the Empire to wait for that adequate organized defence which its commerce, common interests, as well as provincial security require. Even if Intercolonial Federation were indispensable to Imperial Federation, surely the adoption of the latter policy ought not to be delayed during all the years required to mature the former in South Africa; but, as soon as it has been established in Australia, she ought with Canada to be federally organized with the United Kingdom—South Africa coming in as soon as she has arranged her own internal federation, even if she could not join in her present condition; which seems to present no greater obstacles to her being represented in any Council of the Empire that may assemble in London, than it did to her taking part in the Colonial Conference of 1887. It is therefore to be regretted, that the League did not put Intercolonial Federation under its heading of "Measures conducive but not essential in (Imperial) Federation."

On April 13, 1893, a large and influential deputation from the League waited on the Prime Minister to present the report; and the sympathetic reply of Mr. Gladstone—in which he said, "The maintenance of the unity of the Empire and the consolidation of that union is an object dear to us all "—is significant, as indicating the progress of opinion among the leading men of all parties.

The next we hear of the League is, unhappily, its dissolution at the end of 1893. This might, and surely ought to, have been avoided. Even if it were necessary to cut down the office expenditure, a small committee, with an honorary secretary, should have kept the Central League alive, considering that so many branches continue to thrive. But still the death of the League does not affect the life of the cause. There is much in the plea that the principle, having got such a hold, requires no organization to promote it. The Executive put the case for self-destruction at its best, in the following terms:—

"Having elicited from the heads of the two great parties in the State recognition of the supreme importance of the question involved, the League had brought the matter to a point at which it might be and ought to be left in the hands of the Imperial Government. The proposal for a Conference had approved itself to both the late and the present Prime Minister. All that the League could do towards this end would be to continue to press successive Governments to take a step admitted to be desirable, if not essential, and, having regard to the character of its organization, it was more than doubtful whether such pressure would be likely to be effectual. The Committee expressed its confident belief that the interest of all parts of the Empire alike would inevitably demand the solution of the Imperial question, and recorded its profound conviction that the solution reached would be on the lines of Imperial unity, not of disintegration. Whilst recognizing that activity on the part of those specially interested in the various aspects of the question would still be necessary to render effective the aspiration towards national unity which now permeates all classes of the community, the committee expressed its opinion that the Imperial Federation League had reached the limits of its effective action."

A meeting, on November 24, of the Council of the League adopted this report and resolved on dissolution. This seems at least a tactical mistake, as some opponents will, doubtless, attempt to make capital out of it to use against the cause. Here we have another great principle destroying the shell in which it has been hatched.

The Conference of 1887, by which extensive measures for defence were initiated, must be regarded as the first British Imperial representative assembly ever convoked; and the creation of the Australian naval squadron was its great stroke of federal work.

But the question of Imperial Federation was expressly omitted from the consideration of this Conference, which was so federal in its nature and action. The exclusion was a wise and statesmanlike provision; for it was better that the first Conference should give a practical object-lesson in the working of Federation than that it should have discussed the theory. Every one acquainted with the proceedings of the Conference, must recognize that all that was needed to constitute it a federal assembly of the Empire—of a very rudimentary kind, no doubt—was that its sittings should be fixed to take place at regular intervals. Another point practically demonstrated was that by such a Conference the first steps

could best be taken, officially to frame the conditions
of Imperial Federation and to draw up the heads of
a Constitution for the Empire. Before that, however,
is attempted, Conferences may be held for special
purposes, such as the consideration of the question of
commercial treaties with Foreign nations. In fact, if
it were decided that a Conference should take place
every second or third year, there would doubtless be
many important subjects for its consideration.

Besides the illustration furnished by the Conference
of 1887 of the way in which British Federation could
be brought about, when the opinion of the Empire is
ripe for it, we have the example of how the union of
Canada was framed. Mr. Doutre describes it in his
"Constitution of Canada." The first step was taken
by the passing, in 1861, of a resolution by the
Legislature of Nova Scotia, which with those of New
Brunswick and Prince Edward's Island appointed
delegates, in the beginning of 1864, to consider the
union of the Maritime Provinces. In October of the
same year, on the invitation of the Governor-General,
a Convention met at Quebec, to consider the larger
question of Canadian Federation. Ontario and Quebec
were represented by six delegates each, New Brunswick
and Prince Edward's Island by seven each, Nova
Scotia by five, and Newfoundland by two. Seventy-
two resolutions were adopted, only one vote being
allowed to each Province. The Convention sat with
closed doors, and only the results were published.
This is the very opposite of the suggestion that a
Conference, to consider Imperial Federation, should
have cut-and-dried plans prepared for it beforehand.
At first the proposals of the delegates were not
favourably received in the Maritime Provinces, so

that the bill—based on the resolutions of the Convention—introduced to the British Parliament, was limited to Ontario, Quebec, Nova Scotia, and New Brunswick, as the other Provinces were not considered to have sufficiently consented.

We have also very recently had before our eyes the evolution of a scheme of Australian Intercolonial Federation.[1] The first Convention, much like that just referred to, was preceded by a Conference resembling that held in this country in 1887. The bases of union having been agreed upon in Sydney by this preliminary Conference, were approved by all the Australian Parliaments, who also chose delegates to represent them in the Convention. This body, to which the six Australian Colonies appointed seven delegates each, and New Zealand only three, met in Sydney, in March, 1891. It soon drew up the Federal Constitution, which to be established will have to be enacted by the different Parliaments. This has not yet been done, obviously in consequence of the severe financial crisis which so soon after set in throughout Australia.

By a similar process of evolution, an Imperial Federal Constitution would have to be formed. With Intercolonial Federation established in Australia, there would be six Parliaments and Executives concerned in creating the Imperial Federal Union, those of the United Kingdom, Canada, Australia, Cape Colony, Natal, and Newfoundland—the portions of the Empire with self-governing institutions. If, however, Australia should not be federated, the Provincial Governments and Legislatures of the several Colonies

[1] See Mr. Howard Willoughby's "Australian Federation," more extensively referred to at pages 82–84.

would have to take part in the work of framing the
Constitution of the Empire. New Zealand has more
recently declared against entering an Australasian
union, though Imperial Federation has found considerable favour in the Colony.

Although the Crown Colonies might not be asked
to join the Conference and Convention, for the same
reason that they were not invited to the Conference
of 1887—namely, that for the most part their delegates
would be chosen by the Colonial Office—representation
in the Imperial Parliament would have to be given
to them, either separately or in groups, according to
their importance.

The question from whom the proposal to form the
Federal Union should come, is really of little consequence, although some people seem to make a great
deal of it. There are those who would have England
and the Colonies stand, with extreme courtesy bowing
to each other, at the threshold of Federation—like two
over-polite Chinese gentlemen, neither of whom will
take a step forward before the other. Some people
are so dogmatic as to the propriety of the proposal
coming from the Mother Country, whilst others are
as strong in contending that it should be made by the
Colonies, that a difficulty would seem to present itself,
somewhat similar to that which may occur in ordinary
life, if the one of two interesting young persons whose
future welfare may depend upon union, has not the
courage to broach the question. Their happiness then
will altogether depend on whether the other is strong-
minded enough to exercise the privilege which Leap
Year is said to confer. It matters not from whom the
proposal for Federation comes, only that, as it is most
fitting in family life, that the offer for partnership

in his business should be made by the parent to the sons, so the same good feeling would suggest that the offer of partnership—in the great Empire which she has formed, and nourished and protected in its weaker days, for the benefit of them all—should be made by Old Britain to the Young Britains beyond the seas. "The Imperial initiative would be the proper mode of setting to work," as Mr. Gladstone remarked, in concurrence with the deputation from the Imperial Federation League, in April, 1893. It might, therefore, be a standing instruction to all the Governors of the self-governing Colonies, to let it be understood by their Ministers, that the Imperial Government was always open to entertain the question of organized union and partnership in the Empire.

An Imperial Conference—on whichever side proposed—being assembled, would, in order to lay down the bases of a scheme of federation for the consideration of an Imperial Convention, have to declare that—

1. For the promotion of common interests and the maintenance of common defence, it is desirable that a Federal or Confederate Union of the Empire be organized.

2. That it be left to the Convention to say which of these forms of union is preferable, and upon what bases representation should be allotted to all the self-governing dominions of the Empire, and how the Crown Colonies should be admitted, individually or in groups, to the union.

3. That India be under the control of the Imperial Federal Government—to the future consideration and decision of which the question of giving representation to that Empire be left.

4. That an Imperial revenue, to which all parts of the Empire shall equitably contribute, be provided.

5. That all existing rights of Intercolonial Federations and Provincial Self-government, including control of fiscal policy, be fully guaranteed by the Federal Constitution.

6. That an Imperial Convention of representatives of the United Kingdom and self-governing Dominions, and Colonies of the Empire, be assembled in London.

These bases of union would have to be approved, and representatives to the Convention chosen by the various Parliaments. The Convention would then proceed to frame the Constitution, deciding—

1. Whether the union should be a Confederation, in which only the Governments should be represented, or a Federation which would give the people of the Empire the direct election of members to an Imperial Parliament.

2. If a Federation, it would have to decide whether the Parliament should consist of one or two houses, and whether the upper one should be chosen, as in the United States and Germany, to represent the Governments, whilst the lower one should represent the people.

3. It would have to allot the number of members to the British Isles, to each Colonial Dominion, and, where there was no Intercolonial Federation, to each self-governing Colony; but the regulation of the franchise and of the electorates, by which the members should be chosen, could be left to be decided by the respective parliaments.

4. The Convention would have to provide for the representation of the Crown Colonies, giving Malta, Mauritius, and Jamaica a member each, and grouping

the other West Indian Islands and the West African Colonies. None of them might be entitled to representation upon a basis of numerical allotment; but a hard-and-fast rule would have to be avoided, or exceptions made, so as not to leave out of our Imperial system some Colonies, whose population and wealth would always be below any standard that might be fixed. The principle should rather be, to make all our territories and islands feel at home in the Empire, than to apportion federal representation by the Rule of Three.

5. The Imperial Convention would have to define the nature and functions of the Ministry and Executive of the Empire; which would have to include a Premier, ministers of Foreign affairs, War, Marine, and a Law Adviser—a Minister of the interior, if not the Premier, transacting with the Colonial Governments the business now conducted by the Secretary for the Colonies. The Constitution would have to provide that ministers should be responsible to the Parliament, or, as in the United States, hold office for a fixed period; which might be the duration of the Parliament with which they came into power. It could also be provided that no Imperial Ministry should be without an Australian, Canadian, and South African member.

6. The Convention would have to determine the mode of raising an Imperial revenue;[1] either by agreeing that the Parliament of the Empire should have unlimited powers of taxation, or that only upon certain specified sources of revenue, should the Constitution empower it to levy duties, or that it should have no power directly to impose taxes, but only to require the Dominion or Provincial Parliaments to

[1] See pages 193, 199.

contribute subsidies from the revenues raised by them ; or, as in Germany, where the Imperial Legislature has limited powers of taxation, it might be provided that, in case of need, our Parliament of the Empire might resort to subsidies, to supplement any deficiency of revenue, arising from the sources of taxation, to which it was limited by the Constitution, proving inadequate.

7. The Imperial Convention would have to decide what questions would have to be treated by the Constitution as Imperial, and what should remain Provincial. This,[1] we have seen, would not be a matter of much difficulty.

8. Provision would have to be made for the establishment of some Supreme Court, to which, at least, all questions affecting the Imperial Constitution should be referred.

9. An express provision might be put in the Constitution, fully guaranteeing to the Intercolonial Federations and the self-governing Provinces, all their present rights of control over their internal affairs, including tariff and fiscal arrangements—in which they need in no way be restricted, save only as they are at present, in not being allowed to adopt differential duties favouring foreign countries more than those within the Empire. Such a guarantee of Provincial rights would really be superfluous, seeing that any of these which were not expressly limited by the Constitution—which would have to be ratified by the Colonial Parliaments—would continue in full force.

10. A further safeguard would be provided by a provision that any alterations in the Federal Constitution, after establishment, should require similar ratification, or at least to be adopted by three-fourths

[1] See pages 94-114.

of the Dominion Parliaments, that is, by three out of those of the United Kingdom, Canada, Australia, and South Africa.

It is quite possible that at first one of the three last named might remain out of the union, as several of the Canadian Provinces did for a time when the Dominion was established; but it would be possible to begin with the United Kingdom and the two others, or only Canada—whichever remained out, being probably soon drawn in by the benefits and dignity which Imperial Federation would be seen to confer. Were a union established, even only in an elementary form, the confidence in it which would grow from its existence, would doubtless lead to its being rendered more complete, as experience indicated, in what respects it required improvement and development.

That grand structure—our system of free institutions and constitutional governments—which spans the Empire, is rapidly approaching completion. To give it stability, security, and symmetry, the key-stone of Federation will have to be placed in the arch.

CHAPTER XIII.

A FEW CONCLUDING CONSIDERATIONS.

Federation only of value if it confer fiscal and commercial advantages?—Mr. D'Esterre Taylor on Colonies sharing defence of commerce, and advantages of Imperial Federation to that of Australia—Were New South Wales to make Free Trade and Victoria Protection, conditions of joining a British Federation?—Aims of the Imperial Federation League and United Empire Trade League—Intercolonial Federation in Australia and Imperial Federation—Growth of common interests between Canada and Australia—Importance of British Federation to South Africa—Sir Frederick Young on the subject—Australians and independence—Mr. Dalley and Mr. Deakin on Unity of Empire—Effect of Annexation of Canada to United States on question of Imperial Federation—Australia not to separate till she can defend herself—Which division of the Empire shall be greatest in the future, and how it may attain highest splendour—Appointment of Governors, how affecting the Imperial connection and the Provinces themselves—Interchange of Statesmen and officials between different parts of the Empire—The Royal Family in our federal system participating in the benefits of Imperial Federation—Its members as Governors of Provinces —Heirs to the Throne as Viceroys of Intercolonial Federations —Monarchy better suited to the Empire than Republicanism— Title of Sovereign and Empire—Burke's picture of "two extremities" of progress, and that seen by Queen Victoria— Her influence on success of our Constitutional Governments— The first Sovereign of our Federated British Empire.

MANY minor points, and even strong arguments in favour of the policy advocated in this work must be omitted, but there are a few further considerations which can not be passed by without observation.

Something more must be said as to the exceeding

narrowness of the view, which regards Federation as not worth having, unless it can promise direct fiscal and commercial advantages. British Federalists yield to no men in appreciating the value of agreement between all parts of the Empire, as to tariffs and commercial relations, if such a thing can be arrived at ; but they have no sympathy with what may be called the "nothing like leather" view, which makes commerce everything, and, not looking outside the counting-house, fails to see the enormous benefit trade would derive from the security of well-organized Imperial defences, even if Federation could do nothing more for it. But there are people who speak as if they regard union for defence of the Empire and its trade as of little account, if it do not secure greater facilities for direct commercial gain—so vitiated may become the vision from always beholding things through fiscal and commercial spectacles! It would be to safeguard the trade of the Empire that the greater part of the expense of federal defence would have to be incurred.

Mr. H. D'Esterre Taylor, a very able advocate of British Federation in the Colony of Victoria, in a lecture in August, 1893, demonstrated to Australians the vital importance to their commerce of Imperial Federation ; and his arguments are equally conclusive if addressed to the Old Country as well as to all the Colonies. He strongly urges upon the latter their obligation to take a larger share of the expense of joint defence. Beginning, he says that "10 millions of the Empire had no voice in those general questions by which their whole future might be affected. In questions of war they were absolutely without any voice whatever." He goes on to speak of "the commerce of the British Empire amounting to 1200 millions sterling, and out of that some 464 millions was commerce belonging to her Colonies, in which England had no interest;" and he declared that it "was an anomaly," that whilst "one-third of the commerce of the British dominions was commerce in which England's Colonies were interested . . . 19s. 6d. out of every pound for its maintenance and safety was paid by Great Britain, and 6d. by her Colonies."

Mr. Taylor states that "some £60,000,000 of Australian commerce pass across the ocean every year, exclusive of the commerce that goes round our shores. All this goes up to Northern Europe . . . and is as safe as if it were sent from one street to another. And why?" The answer is conclusive for any thoughtful man in Australia—in Old or New Britain—"Because we are part of the Empire. But if we were an independent nation, we would have to look out for ourselves.

*   *   *   *   *   *

"Why the whole of the £60,000,000 of commerce we trade in might be ruined and irreparable injury done to us. The practical experience of independent nations is that they have to establish naval stations wherever they trade, in order to protect their interests. England is an example. How are we to get naval stations in the Northern Hemisphere which will enable us to preserve our interests in this way? And then look at the cost! Why Australia couldn't get a naval station in the Northern Hemisphere at any price, except conquest." (A most important consideration for Australia, newly urged!) "It will, therefore, be for men who advocate separation to find something better than Imperial Federation for the Colonies. Altogether, I think if we were to have a quarrel we should have to

do the same as the Siamese have done—to run away."
And this notwithstanding that Australia, like all other
countries, has her swashbucklers who would rival
those of America, in "whipping all creation!"

Everything tends to show that fiscal and commercial
policy must be left open questions between different
parts of the Empire. Then is Federation hopeless or
undesirable? Suppose New South Wales were to
refuse to join, except on condition of completely retaining her Free Trade policy, and Victoria to decline
unless, in like manner, allowed to have her way in her
own territory with regard to Protection, would it not
be the extreme of folly to reject either of these two
great Colonies? On the contrary, should they not
both be most cordially welcomed into a union of the
Empire as important members, which could add greatly
to its strength, and would be prepared to fulfil all their
federal obligations.

It is too much to expect the speedy adoption of a
uniform fiscal policy, or perhaps that all the self-
governing provinces, and dominions of the Empire will
ever take the same view of politico-economical questions. Nor, however much this might be desirable, is
it indispensable to Imperial Federation, the primary
object of that policy being, by united defence, to assure
peace and security—the most important essentials of
commercial prosperity. The policy of the Imperial
Federation League *plus* that of the United Empire
Trade League may be much the most desirable; but
if we can only have that of the former *minus* that of
the latter, will commercial men decline its advantages?
Our merchants are not so short-sighted as not to
perceive that the security of trade *in*, or *from*, war is of
greater importance than the most perfect fiscal or

commercial arrangements, which an outbreak of hostilities might utterly and for ever derange. The United States have never replaced their mercantile marine, destroyed by a few cruisers during the Civil War. The insurance of perfect defence by land and especially at sea—which Imperial federal organization alone can provide—will be the most valuable boon to the entire commerce of the Empire, however desirable the policy of the Trade League may be. That society will, therefore, do harm if it make the mistake of insisting on its policy being an indispensable condition of Imperial Federation.

It is evident that the question of Intercolonial Federation in Australia will for a time stop the way of Imperial Federation. Any failure of the Australians to federate would retard the latter policy, for it would at first be thought — erroneously, however — that Colonies which could not federate among themselves could not federate with the Empire; although Imperial Federation would require the surrender of far less by the Provincial Governments, and could be worked either with or without Intercolonial Federation. The adoption of Australian Federation would also delay Imperial Federation, for our Australian brothers would have enough to do for a time, in getting their federal institutions into working order. This done, Imperial Federation would come to the front, and could be more easily arranged by four great responsible Governments in the Empire—those of the British Isles, Canada, Australia, and South Africa—than by the much larger number of Governments which, without Intercolonial Federation, would have to deal with the question.

Tendrils of common interest are so frequently throwing themselves out from different branches of the

Empire, and entwining themselves with those stretching from other branches, that pen must be kept
constantly in hand if they are to be noted. This
work was just finished as Mr. Bowell, Canadian
Minister of Trade, and Mr. Sandford Fleming, the
eminent engineer of the Pacific railway, returned from
their important mission to Australia; and it has been
arranged that a conference, which ministers or delegates from that country shall attend, is before long to
be held in Canada, to consider the development of
commerce between the two Great Britains which face
each other in the Pacific. Already a line of steamers
plies between them, and direct telegraphic connection
is likely soon to follow. On no account should the
cable be allowed to touch any but British soil.[1]

The importance of Imperial Federation to Canada
appears throughout this volume, as clearly indispensable to her future existence; that it is the far
most desirable policy for Australia has also been
demonstrated. Its growing value to South Africa has
already been seen; so that even the people of the
Orange Free State, and the Boers in the Transvaal,
may well come to recognize that it will be best for
them to become self-governing Provinces of our great
British union. Sir Frederick Young, who has said
and done so much that is valuable in promoting British
Federation, shows how essential it will be to South
Africa, in words which, for the most part, are of wider
range than even the extensive region to which they
are applied. He says :—[2]

"What is wanted is Imperial Federation, as the goal to be
ultimately reached, to render South Africa politically satisfied

[1] See page 112.
[2] In his " Winter Tour in South Africa," p. 146.

and content. Imperial Federation means a constitutional system, under which she would be no longer misruled and misunderstood, by a Government, in which she has no share."

* * * * * *

"It is not, as is frequently untruly asserted by writers and speakers who have neither studied, comprehended, nor understood its theory and intentions, its end and aim, that it means the subjugation of the independence of the Colonies to the control of the Mother Country. As one of its most earnest" (and he might have added, earliest) "advocates, I emphatically protest against all such erroneous interpretations, as a libel on the principle put forward, as a plan for National Government. On the contrary, the project of Imperial Federation, without any *arrière pensée*, clearly and distinctly involves the condition that the Colonies themselves are to take their adequate part, and share with the Mother Country in its future concrete constitution. In the brief but expressive phrase I have already publicly adopted, Imperial Federation means, 'the Government of the Empire by the Empire.' In Imperial Federation, therefore, South Africa would be fairly and influentially represented, along with the other Colonies of Great Britain. In union with them she would take her part in guiding the policy and directing the destinies of the whole British Empire."

There are, doubtless, some Australians under the delusion that the greatest future for the Island-Continent lies in independence, as there are Canadians and South Africans equally unwise in thinking that the same policy will be best for their respective countries; but no greater aspersion could be cast upon the intelligence and knowledge of the Colonial born than to suppose that many of them are of that opinion. I cannot believe that my Australian fellow-countrymen—whose welfare has always the first place in my heart whenever I advocate Imperial unity and federation—will ever allow themselves to be misled by men, not of Colonial birth, who have been trying to get

into their favour by advocating separation from the
Empire.[1]   Two of the ablest of native-born statesmen
—the late Mr. Dalley, of New South Wales, and Mr.
Deakin, of Victoria—have pronounced in no uncertain
terms in favour of a United Empire, the latter declar-
ing that " to combine in one the dominions of the
British race all the world over," will be the means
of "reaching the highest political organization which
it is possible for us to have, and so to found an Empire the like of which has never been seen in the world
before."

As we have already seen, Sir Henry Parkes has truly
said that in independence Australia would "miss her
higher destiny."   To stand separate from the Empire,
and, isolated, to face great Powers establishing themselves as her neighbours,—France not far off in Asia,
Madagascar and New Caledonia, Russia at Vladivo-
stock, and possibly in the Persian Gulf and even in
India, Germany in New Guinea—may, to romantic or
hot-headed admirers, seem a grand, heroic position for
Australia; but those who love her most, and desire
for her what is best, must regard it as foolish and
Quixotic.   For years she would not have a navy to
prevent one of these Powers from landing sufficient
forces, to appropriate large tracts of her Northern and
North Western territories, nor would she be able to
march troops overland to drive out the invaders.

---

[1] It is remarkable that in Queensland, the youngest of the
Australian Colonies, with the smallest percentage of native-born
population, this idea has perhaps taken most hold.   Whereas in
Canada, where there are so many people, with several generations
of Colonial ancestors, it is extremely weak.   No doubt in Queensland, the most unwise Imperial action, or inaction, respecting
New Guinea, has caused a passing irritation.   It is satisfactory
that the would-be leader of an independence party was so utterly
defeated at the last general election in the Colony.

Saying this no more disparages Australians than the Earl of Chatham's famous words disparaged British soldiers—"I know their virtues and their valour and that they can achieve anything but impossibilities."

A Russian newspaper recently avowed that it is the aim of Muscovite policy to secure an outlet to the Indian Ocean. No doubt it is, even if India be not the ultimate goal of the ambition of Russia; whose acquisition of that country would probably prove of more serious and lasting importance to Australia even than to England. Against such an event both can only find adequate insurance in the organized strength of our federated Empire. With the Colossus of the North striding south, and with the possibility of his coalescing with other Powers or of their maritime forces becoming formidable in her waters, independent Australia would need a much larger navy to safeguard her enormous coast-line, of 8,000 miles, than the British Isles if independent of the Empire, or an independent Canada, or an independent South Africa, or, indeed, any other nation would require to protect its less extensive seaboard. Even compared with her friendly American *vis-à-vis* in the Pacific, Australia, if standing apart from the Empire of Great Britain, would always look to disadvantage, for her people must for ever be greatly outnumbered by those of the United States. The same may be said of Canada, were she to stand an isolated figure beside her great Southern neighbour; and her annexation to that Power would make Imperial Federation of even much more importance to England, Australia, and South Africa, as the only means of preventing them from having the appearance of dwarfs among the nations of the future—high above which must tower the American Union, unless Great Britain federates, and, perhaps, Russia succeeds in colonizing with her people, or otherwise consolidating, the Empire she has acquired by conquest.

For none of our dominions, old or new, can independence of the Empire be desirable, or even safe, for many long years. It needs no prophetic vision, but only a reasonable estimate of the future growth and circumstances of nations, to enable us to affirm, that for Australia—and what follows may almost word for word be said of Canada and South Africa—it would be perilous to become independent before the year 2000; but more probably long afterwards it would be unsafe or undesirable. Were Australia at present willing to enter into that position—which would close some of her brightest prospects, without opening any as good to her—she would stake what now seems her inevitable and most desirable destiny—she would risk the now apparent certainty of political unity, even within her own territories—she would tempt the intrusion of other nations, and might have rooted in her soil communities speaking alien languages. Her future might, easily and for ever, be changed; seeing that for years her condition will be sufficiently plastic to take shape from different moulds. For the sake of the individuality she now desires for herself, if for no other reasons, Australia will do well to secure, on a permanent basis, the organization of her union with the Empire.

It has been cynically suggested that Australia should not think of going out of the Empire, till she can dispense with all aid in the way of defence from England. Were Australians capable of approving of such a policy of meanness, England would be justified in at once leaving them to themselves.

Young communities may, like young persons, pass through a period of existence when they fancy that the most dignified, proud, and enviable position for them is to stand absolutely alone, and without paternal or fraternal help or support, to do everything for themselves. When, however, the years of hobbledehoyhood—which, happily, are few—are past, the advantages of association and partnership with those nearest of kin are fully appreciated. The good sense, high education, political and general, of the great majority of native-born Australians will, doubtless, restrain any minority from placing their country in any absurd or objectionable position—will prevent them from tolerating an undignified spread-eagleism and falling into provincial narrowness—and will clearly demonstrate to them, as to people in all parts of the Empire, that the dignity, development, security, and self-government of its greatest, as well as of its least important dominions, will be best sustained and safeguarded by well-organized Imperial unity. Whether England, Canada, Australia, or South Africa shall be the greatest in the future—and to whatever height of national splendour she may rise—her position in the world will be grander, safer, more peaceful and dignified, as a member of the United Empire of Great Britain, than as the greatest fragment of that mighty Power if, unhappily, it were broken in pieces.

The question of the appointment of Governors is of great importance, whether regarded as affecting the relations of the Colonies with the Mother Country, or of the Intercolonial Federation with its Provinces, or in its effect on these individually. The great link, until Federation produces a much greater, between the Imperial Government and the Colonies is the

Governor appointed by the Crown. Since the establishment of the Canadian Union, the Governor-General is the only one of these links remaining with British Federal America, the Provincial Governors being appointed by the Dominion Executive. In the plan of Australian Federation, approved by the Convention of 1891, it is provided that the Governor-General shall be appointed by the Queen, but that the Parliaments of each of the Federated Provinces shall be left to decide how their respective Governors shall be chosen; so that the present system may still be continued. This, from every point of view, seems the most desirable, being certainly most so for the Provinces themselves. With systems of constitutional government, such as obtain in our Empire, worked by political parties, the Governor, the representative of the Queen, should be as free from all suspicion of party partiality as her Majesty herself has always been. This cannot be if the Governor be selected in the Colony, either by its Parliament or by popular vote. During his term of office, the man who ought to hold high and evenly the constitutional scales however fairly he might try to do so, would be regarded by the party vanquished by him at his election, as a triumphant opponent. This is objectionable enough in the States, where our system of changing ministers, when the majority in the popular Chamber goes against them, does not exist. How much worse it would be with us had we elected Governors! They would not infrequently have to call upon the party opposed to theirs to form a cabinet, and then the Prime Minister, the chief adviser of the Governor, would perhaps be the very man who had been the chosen champion of the opposite party in the contest with him for the governorship.

Whatever might be his decision, when asked to grant a dissolution, would be embarrassing for him. He would be sure to be accused of looking to the interests of his political friends; or, from extreme conscientiousness, he might adopt the alternative least desirable for the country, by inclining, with an excess of impartiality, the scales to the side of his opponents. Socially—and this is a most important consideration as to the head of the State under our constitutional systems—however personally acceptable he and his wife might be, a Governor, selected from among the party statesmen of a Colony, could never be as generally acceptable and become so widely popular, as most of the governors sent from England for many years have been.

But it may be contended that such a fine piece of patronage as the Provincial Governorship ought not to be withheld from the Parliament of the Province, or, at least, from the Executive of the Intercolonial Federation, to which it belongs, and certainly ought to be reserved as a splendid prize for the laudable ambition of Provincial public men. It may be remarked, in passing, that to them a well-organized Federation of the Empire would open up greater and more numerous prizes. Considerations of patronage and premiums for individuals, however regarded by professional politicians, are small compared to those affecting the best interests of the state. To gratify the Provincial Parliament with a great exercise of patronage, and also to satisfy individual ambitions, a hundred times in a century—were the election of Governor annual, or twenty times were it, as it would be sure to be, every five years—would be mere dust in the balance, compared to the importance to the scores of millions of people, who in a hundred years would be concerned in having the head man of their Province selected in the best possible manner. It is, therefore, mainly on their account that the continuation of the present mode of appointing Governors is to be preferred. As Mr. Willoughby puts it—from the Colonial point of view, in his well-weighed consideration of the question, in which he inclines to the existing system —" The difference of opinion as to the right policy to be pursued, whether to make the Governorship of the Colony a local or an Imperial appointment, will occur, not in England, but in Australia itself." Whenever the question may arise of the Transvaal and Orange Free State coming into the Empire, there would be no reason, with Imperial Federation, why they should not retain the election of their presidents, should they prefer it.

Looking solely to the interests of the Provinces in the question, it is impossible to suggest a better system than selection of Governors by the Crown. It is free from the worst objections which can be urged against hereditary monarchs and elected presidents. The connection of the Provinces with the Empire can, however, be perfectly maintained without it, as we see in the instance of Canada. With the establishment of Imperial Federation, it would not be England that would make the appointments, but the Sovereign, on the advice of the Federal Ministry, in which the Colonies would be well represented. The Provincial Governors would have little or no business to transact with the Imperial authorities, where there was an Intercolonial Federation, as they would be under its Governor-General.

Were British Federation established, it might be

desirable for Canada to restore to the Imperial Government the appointment of the Provincial Governors, for the reasons above assigned, and also for others of importance. It would be well, under a federal system, to provide for a considerable interchange of officials and public men between the different portions of the Empire; so that those who should have to conduct its central government should have as extensive an acquaintance as possible with its various territories. It would also be of great advantage to these that they should have among their public and official men, those who could bring back to them experience derived from having served for a time in other parts of the Empire. Canadians as well as Englishmen might well go as Governors to Australia and Australians to Canada. It is to be hoped too, that public men, starting in the Provinces—and rising to the Inter-colonial Federal Parliament, and then to that of the Empire, or even taken direct from their own Provinces—would be made Governors of the Presidencies, and even Viceroys of India. The Colonial constitutional systems, though not yet long in existence, have produced men quite equal to the highest of these positions.

To avoid invidious mention of living men, two recently dead may without hesitation be named—Sir Alexander Galt and Sir John Macdonald. With Crown Colony Governorships also open to public men from the self-governing Colonies, these would gain more than they would lose by leaving the appointment of their governors with the Imperial Ministry; and then the Diplomatic and Consular services of the Federated Empire would be open to statesmen and officials from all its parts. Even now, young men from the Colonies can compete for these, as also for the Home and Indian Civil

Services and the Army and Navy; and it would only be necessary that some greater facilities should be afforded them for preparing and going in for the required examinations.

The Royal Family, in common with the whole British race and nation, would feel the beneficial and brilliant effects of Imperial Federation. The sphere of its occupations, and of its usefulness might be greatly extended, by its members being brought into constant, advantageous, and agreeable contact with the people in all our Dominions. This they would be by holding Governorships as well as military and naval positions among them. Nothing could be more fitting than that, at times, the sons and brothers of the Sovereign should be Viceroys of the Canadian, Australian, and South African Federations. Even an heir-apparent to the throne of the Empire, although he might not be able to serve for the full term of governorship, might do so for a time. The Duke of York might take the position in Canada for perhaps two years—even for one would be better than that he should never occupy it; and then, were a union formed in Australia, he might also preside over that. No arrangement could be more happy than that he should go out as first Viceroy, on the inauguration of Intercolonial Federation in Australia. What a splendid apprenticeship it would be, for a future monarch of the great Constitutional Empire of Great Britain, to preside over the free Parliamentary Governments of its two greatest Dominions! Our princes would be trained to take their most useful parts in our federal systems; and there is no reason why, if the appointment of Colonial Governors be left with the Imperial Government, they should not take

Provincial Governorships as well as Viceroyalties, especially as the individual Colonies become more populous and important.

It would be narrow prejudice to say that Republicanism has not many merits, and is not the best form of government for some peoples—the French, for example. For our Empire, however, Monarchy, even were it not the existing form of government, will have the greatest advantages. It will impart to it greater dignity, in many ways. It would be preferable, were it only to save us from a periodical scramble for the chieftainship of the nation, between rival candidates, with months of noise, abuse, exaggeration, and party trickery. No doubt the nuisance might be abated in America, by having the President elected by the Chambers, as in France.

It is impossible to estimate the immense good our Royal Family could do, not merely socially, but nationally, in moving about among all our people throughout the Federated Empire. Its head, the Sovereign, and Royal Family, would be felt to belong as much to Australians, Canadians, South Africans, as to the people of the British Isles—just as much as the Federal Parliament in which they would all be directly represented.

There is much in a name. What should be the official name of the Empire, and the title of its Sovereign would therefore be important. "Queen of Great Britain" would be most desirable; but the words "and Ireland," which now form part of the title, limit it geographically to these Isles. Mr. Forster—with whom I once had the advantage of a conversation on the subject—did not think it would be easy to get over this difficulty, as to the use of

"Great Britain." Neither England, Wales, nor Scotland is named in the title, having to be content to be included in "Great Britain," whilst Ireland stands alone in solitary distinction. If, however, she would not be aggrieved, at being included with the rest of the Empire in the term "Great Britain," it could easily be defined—by Act of Parliament or Royal Proclamation, or both—to apply to the whole Federated Empire; so that, in addition to the names of the United Kingdoms, of Canada, Australia, and South Africa, it could be printed across all our maps. Whatever name for the Empire may be decided upon, the same word or words should include all the countries inhabited by our race. "Britain" would not need the "Great" before it, for the fact would be so very obvious were the Empire federated. Perhaps the insertion of the words "of the Realms of" between "Queen" and "Britain" or "Great Britain" would get over the difficulty about Ireland—the British Isles, Australia, Canada, and South Africa, being each defined to be one of the Realms of Britain.

"It is good for us to be here," exclaimed Burke in admiration of the much less remarkable progress of the Empire of his day. "We stand where we have an immense view of what is and of what is past. Let us, however, before we descend from this noble eminence, reflect that this growth of our national prosperity has happened within the short period of the life of man. There are those alive whose memory might touch the two extremities." In no age or country did the memory of any Sovereign touch two extremities, of progress so remarkable, as that witnessed during her reign by Queen Victoria. Among men and monarchs she has occupied a unique position, as a witness of the most marvellous panorama, the most striking transformation-scene, which could ever have been presented—and but once—to human sight. When her Majesty came to the throne, the Colony now bearing her name, and also South Australia, consisted of tiny settlements only a few months old; a mere handful of white men had pushed as far as the borders of what is now Queensland; New Zealand had no existence as a Colony till some years later; South Africa was in a most backward condition. No visionary had then even dreamed of the opening of telegraphic communication with Australia, or that men would be able to travel, in a fortnight, from London to the Pacific shores of Canada. Only till death sheathed the sword of the Great Alexander, and till defeat shattered that of the Great Napoleon, did the Empires endure which their mighty deeds of war had carved out. But the peaceful Empire, raised up under the gentle sceptre of Queen Victoria, has every appearance of being lasting and beneficent. It only requires, for its perfect establishment, united organization of its common defence and joint concerns. It possesses all the advantages of complete self-government in all its Dominions peopled by Britons.

It should be more fully recognized how much the success of constitutional self-government, in so many Colonies, is due to its inauguration under the auspices and example of the most perfect constitutional Sovereign that ever presided over a free people. Her reign is now so nearly the longest in the annals of England, that we may hope it will become so by many years. Considering how the Colonial Empire has risen under her Majesty's rule—above all the important influence she has exercised in the constitutional de-

velopment of its free institutions—what would be more
fitting than that the Colonies should, under her, be
welded together, with each other and with Old England,
in permanent federal union—that she should be the first
Sovereign, Queen of Britain or Great Britain—a united
world-wide Empire of free, self-governing States,
perfectly organized for their common welfare, into
the greatest of Powers. Should such a Queen not be
the first of a long line of its federal Sovereigns, history
will regretfully record the fact.

APPENDIX.

I VENTURED to suggest the following plan of Imperial Military Organization—which might even be adopted before Federation —to the War Office, and subsequently in a letter, published in *The Colonies and India*, on March 14, 1888.

The territorial system, as far as this country is concerned, has been carried out with regard to the British army. Why should it not be carried further? and by its extension to the Colonies they would, for this practical purpose, become expansions of England—" So many Kents," as Professor Seeley has so well expressed the great idea of national identity. If each important Colony were to have its own regiment of Imperial regulars—or the larger Colonies might even have more than one—we should have the New South Wales (or 1st and 2nd) Regiment, the Victoria Regiment, the Ontario Regiment, the New Zealand Regiment, the Cape Regiment, of Imperial troops on the same footing as the Kent or Middlesex Regiments. The details would be a mere matter of military organization, to be arranged between the Imperial army authorities and the Colonial Governments.

When Imperial troops were withdrawn from Australia, the Colonies were willing to have retained them at their own expense, if the Mother Country had undertaken not to remove them in time of war. This was not unreasonable; and it should be provided that, if Imperial forces are to be again maintained by Canada, South Africa, or Australia, a certain number of them shall always be retained in those parts of the Empire—no Province or Colony supporting an Imperial regiment being ever left without one, except when it might be expedient to concentrate the Imperial forces within the respective limits of the countries named.

In order, however, that these regiments should be thoroughly efficient—so as to furnish standards of perfection for the Colonial Militias and Volunteers, as well as to be Imperial in *esprit de corps* and in all other respects—it would be necessary that each of them should pass one year out of every three or four, brigaded with other Imperial forces either in this country or in India. The expense of thus moving the troops would only consist of the cost of the coal, and of the crews of the transports employed in conveying the regiments, for the soldiers would have to be fed wherever they were. A ship, in going for any Imperial regiment in the Colonies, would have to take out another to put in its place.

The only serious difficulty, suggested to me by a military authority, is that, if regiments with higher rates of Colonial pay, were brigaded with other troops, these latter would become discontented. But surely there would be ways of getting over this difficulty. Men on enlisting in the Colonial Imperial regiments, could have impressed on them, as a distinct condition of the service, that they would only receive the same pay as other Imperial troops whenever brigaded with them in England or India; or the difference between the two rates of pay might be kept back during the brigading period, and be handed over to the men on leaving the service. The Imperial troops from the Colonies would thus have no more to spend than their comrades.

Ultimately, if not immediately, sufficient recruits, for the Imperial regiments with Colonial territorial designations, would be found among the Colonial youth, for in every country a military life has the strongest attractions for many young men; but the recruiting field of a regiment should never be limited to the territory to which it belonged. To maintain the Imperial character of our British army, it would be undesirable that any of its regiments should draw its men or officers exclusively from any particular part of the Empire. But each Colony supporting an Imperial regiment should have, at least, as many of its sons holding commissions, in various regiments and divisions of the Imperial army, as would be required to officer a regiment. A corresponding number of nominations for commissions should, therefore, be assigned to each Colony maintaining an Imperial regiment.

Thus, with a little expansion of its organization, the British army would be more thoroughly Imperial than it has ever been, and its efficiency for the defence of the Empire would be greatly increased. If each province in Canada and Australia had, in addition to its Militia and Volunteer Forces, an Imperial regiment of a thousand men, these portions of the Empire would be almost absolutely secure from military attack; for, within a few days, by means of the Pacific Railway, an Imperial army of five or six thousand regular troops could be concentrated on the western shores of the dominion to repel any force which could be landed from beyond the sea. In Australia, also, with their systems of railways, the four Colonies on the mainland could in a few days concentrate four thousand Imperial regulars. Sydney and Melbourne are considered to be completely defended from naval attack; but only the Colonial governments and the eminent Imperial military authorities whom they have consulted, can say whether they are perfectly safe against an enemy who might land two or three thousand men on the coast, beyond the range of the harbour forts, and march upon either capital from the rear. Any such danger, or the holding of any position on the Australian coast, by any force which could be brought from beyond the sea, ought to be, and I submit would be, rendered impossible by such Imperial organization as I venture to suggest.

Besides being periodically brigaded with other Imperial regulars in other parts of the Empire, the Imperial troops in Canada and in Australia could, by means of the railway systems, be respectively brought together, every alternate year or so, for manœuvres, in which the Militias and Volunteers might take part, to the more perfect training of both regular and reserve forces.

This extension of Imperial military organization to the Colonies would facilitate the raising in them of considerable armies, if serious danger to any of our territories or to the Empire at large should ever require them.

The Commander-in-Chief, some time since, expressed regret

that the Colonies had been altogether deprived of the presence
of Imperial troops. It is most desirable that Britons of Colonial
birth should always have some of these among them, which
they could call their own. It may be that the Imperial sentiment was first kindled in me by the sight of a few British
redcoats, whom I can distinctly remember seeing, when I was
a very little child, marching through the streets of my native
city, Melbourne.

Very similar arrangements might be made as regards war
vessels maintained by the Colonies, like those of the Australian
squadron.

INDEX.

LONDON : PRINTED BY WILLIAM CLOWES AND SONS, LIMITED,
STAMFORD STREET AND CHARING CROSS.

www.ingramcontent.com/pod-product-compliance
Lightning Source LLC
Chambersburg PA
CBHW020513270326
41926CB00008B/852